The MBA Compass

Bodo B. Schlegelmilch • George D. Iliev

The MBA Compass

Finding Your True North in the Maze of MBA Programs

Bodo B. Schlegelmilch
Institute for International Marketing Management
Vienna University of Economics and Business
Vienna, Austria

George D. Iliev
Association of MBAs (AMBA)
London, UK

ISBN 978-3-031-42738-1   ISBN 978-3-031-42739-8   (eBook)
https://doi.org/10.1007/978-3-031-42739-8

© The Editor(s) (if applicable) and The Author(s), under exclusive license to Springer Nature Switzerland AG 2023

This work is subject to copyright. All rights are solely and exclusively licensed by the Publisher, whether the whole or part of the material is concerned, specifically the rights of translation, reprinting, reuse of illustrations, recitation, broadcasting, reproduction on microfilms or in any other physical way, and transmission or information storage and retrieval, electronic adaptation, computer software, or by similar or dissimilar methodology now known or hereafter developed.

The use of general descriptive names, registered names, trademarks, service marks, etc. in this publication does not imply, even in the absence of a specific statement, that such names are exempt from the relevant protective laws and regulations and therefore free for general use.

The publisher, the authors, and the editors are safe to assume that the advice and information in this book are believed to be true and accurate at the date of publication. Neither the publisher nor the authors or the editors give a warranty, expressed or implied, with respect to the material contained herein or for any errors or omissions that may have been made. The publisher remains neutral with regard to jurisdictional claims in published maps and institutional affiliations.

This Springer imprint is published by the registered company Springer Nature Switzerland AG
The registered company address is: Gewerbestrasse 11, 6330 Cham, Switzerland

Paper in this product is recyclable.

Appraisals
"A reflective and compelling book offering profound insights for learners from around the world with various backgrounds and experiences while choosing the MBA program that best suits their lifelong learning objectives and career path and can help them realize their ambitions and future aspirations. It is a must-read for today's fresh graduates, mid-career planners, entrepreneurs, and future leaders from different walks of life who want to make a difference in an increasingly innovation-driven, hypercompetitive, and changing global marketplace. For those who are interested in better understanding the continuously transformative market for MBA degrees coupled with the impact graduate innovative business and management education can have on society, *The MBA Compass: Finding Your True North in the Maze of MBA Programs* serves as an invaluably relevant, timely and informative reference."
　—Sherif Kamel, *Dean, School of Business, Vice Chair of the AACSB Board, The American University in Cairo, Egypt*

"The MBA continues to be not only the flagship programme for most business schools around the world, but is also the most recognised academic business qualification worldwide. Bodo and George are two of the world's leading experts on all MBA issues, offering a truly global perspective on one of the most important investment decisions an ambitious business student will make in their lifetime."
　—Andrew Main Wilson, *CEO, AMBA & BGA, London, UK*

"MBA candidates find themselves stranded on the quest to find the right MBA. Through this book, management education experts offer you a compass that will steer you in the right direction for your life-changing MBA."
—Hiroyuki Kurimoto, *Chancellor, NUCB Business School, Nagoya, Tokyo, Osaka, Japan*

"This book is an indispensable guide for anyone considering an MBA, whether they are relatively fresh graduates, experienced managers, or aspiring entrepreneurs. With its comprehensive sections on finding the right MBA, making the most of your studies, and reaping long-term benefits, this book offers invaluable insights and practical advice. Written by seasoned experts in the field, it provides (in)credible recommendations that will help you confidently navigate the complex world of MBA programs."
—Steef L van de Velde, *Former Dean of Rotterdam School of Management, Erasmus University, The Netherlands*

"Are you still wondering whether or not you should pursue an MBA degree? Still confused about which program is right for you, but you don't know where to find information nor have time to search for it? This book is for you! It gets the job done for you to decide better and get more value out of an MBA degree."
—Lailani L. Alcantara, *Dean of the School of Management, Ritsumeikan Asia Pacific University, Beppu, Japan*

"Bodo and George produced a fantastic work to help prospective students make the important decision engaging in an MBA journey. The depth and perspective of their work also can help schools to improve and redesign their programs. A necessary read for all involved with MBAs."
—Luiz Artur Ledur Brito, *Dean, Fundação Getulio Vargas—EAESP, São Paulo, Brazil*

"What a fantastic navigator for finding the right MBA program! This is a must-read for future leaders considering an MBA program for leveraging their career."
—Gunther Friedl, *Dean of the School of Management, Technical University of Munich (TUM), Germany*

"Finding your way through the complex landscape of MBA programs can be overwhelming, but *The MBA Compass* is the ultimate tool to guide you. With its practical insights and expert advice, this book equips aspiring students with the

necessary direction to make informed decisions. A must-read for anyone embarking on their MBA journey."
—Christian Andres, *Dean of WHU, Otto Beisheim School of Management, Koblenz, Germany*

"*The MBA Compass* written by our Bualuang ASEAN Chair Professor Bodo Schlegelmilch and his co-author George Iliev is an invaluable guide for aspiring MBAs, entrepreneurs, and experienced managers alike. With its comprehensive coverage of topics ranging from choosing the right MBA program to maximizing the long-term benefits of your degree, this book provides the compass you need to navigate the complex world of business education and achieve your career goals."
—Gasinee Witoonchart, *Member of the EFMD Board, Rector of Thammasat University, Bangkok, Thailand*

"The book draws on a combination of extensive, international data and the authors' outstanding academic experience to provide a comprehensive depiction and evaluation of the MBA journey. A must for both potential MBA candidates and staff and faculty of business schools."
—Salvador Carmona, *Rector and Dean of Faculty, IE Business School, Madrid, Spain*

"This book, like its authors, is data-driven, clear and able to guide the professional path of all who want to expand their professional opportunities."
—Veneta Andonova Zuleta, *Dean, Universidad de los Andes School of Management, Colombia*

"The best first step to decide on an MBA Program is to ask those scholars and teachers for advice who really know a lot about MBAs. You learn from those who have organized and directed excellent programs and who have attained teaching experience in schools all over the world. This book summarizes the authors' comprehensive expertise."
—Christoph Badelt, *Former Rector of WU Vienna, Member of the EFMD Board, President of the Austrian Fiscal Advisory Council and the Austrian Productivity Board, Austria*

"An MBA education can be a huge career booster for the right people at the right time. This book by Bodo Schlegelmilch and George Iliev is a savior for those considering an MBA program. Its comprehensive analysis can guide you through the maze of the numerous MBA programs available out there, and once you have landed at the right program, the book provides you with tips that help you make the most out of the program. And the help does not end there, because the book goes on to lay out the lifetime value of an MBA program, even long after you have graduated. If you care about the return from your investment in an MBA program, this is the book you must read, carefully!"
—Fangruo Chen, *Dean, Antai College of Economics and Management, Shanghai Jiao Tong University, China*

"*The MBA Compass* is a key tool that supports the MBA journey, from selection process and navigating trade-offs across different schools and programs, to providing insightful post-MBA advice. It's more than just a book, it is indeed your personal compass for success through the MBA world."
—Francisco Veloso, *Dean, Imperial College Business School, London, UK and Incoming Dean, INSEAD, France/Singapore*

"In a world of so many business schools this books helps students, alumni, and stakeholders make sense of the landscape. Schlegelmilch and Iliev provide a tour de force of the diversity, sector standards, and offerings across business schools while demonstrating that a good quality MBA remains a key lever for aspiring leaders across the world."
—Mark Smith, *Director, Stellenbosch Business School, Stellenbosch, South Africa*

"This book provides an excellent guide for students and business people considering the possibility of studying for a masters degree in business administration (MBA). The discussion moves with the reader in considering first whether the degree is a good career option, and then deciding where to study and in which format, all the way to looking at long-term career impacts of the MBA experience. The discussion comes from two professionals with extensive experience teaching in MBA programs, organizing them, accrediting them, and dealing with companies that recruit from them. A valuable tool for decision making by people interested in pursuing business studies at the graduate level."

—Robert Grosse, *Former Dean, EGADE Business School, Monterrey Tec; Former Dean, American University of Sharjah, Professor of International Business, Thunderbird School of Global Management (Arizona State University), USA*

"Bodo and George have created a superb guide to the MBA degree. Based on their exceptional expertise as both educators and administrators of MBA programs around the world, they provide an informative, comprehensive, and insightful roadmap to getting an MBA. Having such clear advice on all essential questions surrounding this major career undertaking—from choosing a program that fits best to one's skills and aspirations, to navigating effectively through the program for maximum benefit, while also considering the lifelong impact of an MBA degree, is invaluable, especially when it is offered by such globally respected experts in graduate business education."
—Tatiana Kostova, *Carolina Distinguished Professor and Buck Mickel Endowed Chair, Darla Moore School of Business, South Carolina, USA*

"In today's knowledge economy, an individual's formal education, professional experience, and intellectual capital provides the essential foundation for continued opportunity and success. The MBA is a valuable way to enhance business acumen and deepen leadership capability, but, which MBA? Making a decision over the choice of country, business school, and type of MBA can be difficult and overwhelming. *The MBA Compass: Finding your True North in the Maze of MBA Programs*, written by leading global experts in business education provides a timely and comprehensive guide for anyone considering an MBA. If you are serious about investing in your MBA, then investing in this book will help you make an informed decision."
—Amanda Gudmundsson, *Executive Dean, Faculty of Business and Law, Queensland University of Technology, Australia*

"*The MBA Compass* fills a much-needed gap in every potential student's MBA journey, by helping students make better decisions about which MBA programs might be right for them. Schlegelmilch and Iliev, with their extensive experience of a wide variety of MBA programs around the world, do a wonderful job of bringing clarity to the differences across programs, which anyone considering an MBA would be well-advised to heed. The book also appeals to business school and university leaders by providing a comprehensive view of the state of MBA

education. I believe this book is a must-read in the MBA space for students, faculty, and deans!"
—Srilata Zaheer, *Former Dean, Carlson School of Management and Elmer L. Andersen Chair in Global Corporate Social Responsibility, University of Minnesota, USA*

Foreword by Professor John A. Quelch

The MBA market is cluttered. Demand has ballooned in the last forty years as globalization brought free market thinking and improved prosperity to countries previously off-limits to capitalism. At the same time, barriers to entry are low. A college or university in need of extra revenues can easily establish an MBA program without any capital investment. In many jurisdictions, accreditation is important but not compulsory.

There are over 16,000 institutions worldwide offering business degrees. An MBA degree is, almost like Coca-Cola, within an arm's reach of desire. Choice can improve access and spawn innovation. But, in the case of the MBA degree, quality is inevitably highly variable. Buyers must beware of charlatans, imposters, and outright fraud.

Choosing the right program for you requires careful research and planning. Chasing a brand name is no more likely to lead to a good outcome than choosing the lowest cost program. Remember that the institution you choose will be on your resume for life; very few people can afford the opportunity cost of taking a second MBA at a better institution. Moreover, colleges and universities usually collect your tuition in advance, making dropping out expensive. There are significant risks to making a suboptimal choice.

That's why The MBA Compass is so valuable and important. It provides a roadmap to guide these important decisions; whether or not an MBA is a good investment for you at this stage of your career; and, if yes, how to choose the program that will give you the greatest return on your investment, given your career ambitions, location preferences, and finances.

In recent years, the traditional two-year residential MBA degree has become somewhat less fashionable. We have seen a proliferation of one-year specialist Masters programs in Finance, Business Analytics, and other subjects. While these courses are often rigorous, they do not teach business administration. They do not offer the necessary breadth of subject matter from accounting to strategy to human behavior that is essential to effective management and leadership. A good MBA program will offer an integrated, general management curriculum with several real-world team projects, supervised by experienced faculty. Do not accept mediocre programs offering anything less.

In addition to the quality, completeness, and innovativeness of the MBA curriculum, it is important to look at the faculty and at the students. I recently reviewed the tenured faculty of a business school with eighty professors, of whom only four had earned MBAs. The rest held PhDs in statistics, economics, and psychology, had never managed a payroll, and probably never walked a factory floor. No doubt some of their MBA graduates go on to good careers but I doubt that the MBA program has added much to their managerial and leadership potential. My message here is look at the profiles of the faculty who will teach you, not just the glossy brochure with the appealing course names.

It is also important, if you can, to visit the schools you are considering. Ask to sit in on a class. You can observe the competence and dedication of the students as well as the faculty. You need to see students who are engaged, students who seem better than you, and from whom you will therefore learn as much as from the faculty. A coherent, supportive alumni network in the geographies where you expect to work can help your career path and should therefore play a role in your decision process.

I recently searched the Internet for quotations about MBAs. Many are disparaging critiques of the know-it-all MBA who expects staff to do all the work. I noted that these quotes are delivered by people who don't have MBAs and proud to have succeeded regardless. Or perhaps they have had poor experiences by hiring MBAs from institutions lacking faculty committed to providing a practical, integrated general management education replete with team projects, simulations, and experiential learning.

In choosing the right MBA program, you are not flying blind. There are three important international accreditation bodies that certify that business schools have met baseline standards. These are the American AACSB, the European EQUIS, and the British AMBA (which certifies MBA programs specifically rather than business schools in general). You are more likely to receive a good return on your investment if you choose an MBA program with at least one of these certifications.

But beyond relying on an agency stamp of approval, you should also read The MBA Compass by Bodo Schlegelmilch and George Iliev, both dedicated business school professionals with deep, global knowledge of the MBA market. Their unique contribution is to guide your personal MBA decision-making process so that you can choose the program that is right for you.

Boston, MA, USA, June 4, 2023   John A. Quelch

To the Reader

A Master of Business Administration (MBA) carries prestige and signals competence and success. MBA graduates (also referred to as MBAs) are widely credited with sharp analytical skills, business shrewdness, and excellent communication skills. Accordingly, for freshly minted Bachelors and professionals at the beginning of their career, an MBA degree is often seen as a pathway to the upper echelons of management and higher pay.

However, increasingly professionals with years of management experience also turn to MBA programs to update their knowledge and sharpen their leadership skills. Managers who started their career as engineers, IT professionals, chemists, biologists, or in any other non-business related function and were later promoted into various leadership roles, have a particular need to place their management skills on a more solid footing through pursuing an MBA.

Then, there are the entrepreneurs who aim to develop their business idea into a sustainable venture. Right from the start, they need to focus not only on the product or service idea on which they want to build their business, but also learn about raising funds, managing budgets, leading people, and finding customers. An MBA program can guide entrepreneurs through this process.

Given the different motivations and backgrounds of potential MBA applicants, it is obvious that the requirements applicants place on MBA programs differ. Not everyone needs an MBA from Harvard or Stanford, not everyone needs a two-year full-time MBA, and not everyone needs to pursue a degree by physically attending an MBA program. In fact, you may be better off pursuing alternative management education options altogether. While an MBA degree is usually the prestige flagship program of a business school, more specialized Master of Science (MSc) programs or non-degree executive courses may serve your needs better than an MBA program. Depending on your first degree, your prior managerial experience and your objectives, you may even wish to consider a Doctor of Business Administration (DBA).[1]

This book aims to guide you in your decision-making, whether you are a fresh Bachelor graduate, an entrepreneur, or an experienced manager. It is divided into three sections:

- Finding and applying for the right MBA
- Making the most of your MBA studies
- Benefiting from the long-term value of your MBA

Finding and Applying for the Right MBA: In Chap. 1, we start by looking at the motivations for pursuing MBAs. This will help you decide whether an MBA is really for you. In Chap. 2, we turn to the selection of suitable Business Schools and MBA programs. This is a difficult topic. Estimates vary between 13,000 and 16,000 institutions in the world granting business degrees,[2] and good programs are no longer only located in Europe or the USA. On the contrary, excellent business schools and MBA programs can be found in China, India, Latin America, and many other countries and regions throughout the globe. Chapter 3 is entirely devoted to the important role of accreditations and rankings in choosing an MBA program. Next, Chaps. 4 and 5 disentangle the application process; first by scrutinizing what business schools look for in an MBA candidate, and second, how a candidate should apply for an MBA program.

Making the Most of Your MBA Studies: Once you are in an MBA program, you should extract the most academic value from the selected program. This is the focus of Chap. 6. However, good MBA programs offer much more than academic value. Think, for example, about extracurricular activities, such as sports clubs or networking events. During an MBA program, you will also be given opportunities to take various personality tests to develop your self-awareness, sharpen your interview skills, or receive mentoring. These and other benefits that go beyond the academic content of an MBA program are discussed in Chap. 7.

---

[1] Kalika and Platt (2022).
[2] The Economist (2011); AACSB (2023).

Benefiting from the Long-Term Value of Your MBA: Chapter 8 illustrates how an MBA program can boost your career. Again, this differs depending on whether you are a management novice or already an experienced executive. In Chap. 9, we focus on alumni associations. They can play an important role, ranging from facilitating contacts that help you find your first (or a better) job, to organizing continuous learning events and as contact brokers for developing new business opportunities. Finally, Chap. 10 invites you to think long term and reflect on the potential impact of your MBA. These considerations may also inform the choice of your MBA program and, consequently, connect back to the very beginning of the book, i.e., the reason for pursuing an MBA.

Before delving into these topics, we need to reveal our bias. As we are part of the global Association of MBAs (AMBA), we see an MBA program as a postgraduate degree with a general management focus, i.e., not a functionally specialized program such as an MSc. Furthermore, we believe that an MBA offers most value to students who already have some management experience. Thus, we favor MBA programs that require at least some business experience of admitted applicants.

This leaves the question: why you should trust our view? This is the part where we blow our own trumpets! We both have considerable experience in the MBA "market" from multiple perspectives: as the Chairman of AMBA, former business school dean, and professor, who taught MBAs and executive programs in more than 30 countries; and as Director of MBA Accreditation at AMBA, who obtained two MBA degrees after studying in Europe, America, and Asia and who has managed the accreditation/re-accreditation of around 1000 MBA programs in nearly 200 MBA accreditation visits on six continents. Taken collectively, we trust that this background gives us the credibility to make meaningful recommendations to you, on how to find a suitable MBA program and we are confident that you can benefit from our perspectives.

References

Kalika, M. and Platt, S. (2022). The Doctor of Business Administration*: Taking your professional practice to the next level.* Cobham: IEDP | Ideas for Leaders Ltd.

The Economist. (2011, October 15). *Trouble in the middle: Is time running out for business schools that aren't quite elite? The Economist.* Accessed May 3, 2023, from https://www.economist.com/briefing/2011/10/15/trouble-in-the-middle.

AACSB (2023), Worldwide Business Schools Estimate of 16,565 Institutions - by Rogert Colin Nelson, AACSB Senior Manager of Data Analysis, May 1, 2023.

Contents

Part I Finding and Applying for the Right MBA

1 Why Would You Want an MBA — 3
  Check Your Rationale — 3
  Explore the Psychographics — 9
  Find Your Ikigai — 10
  Embrace the Challenges — 11
  Manage Your Time — 13
  Summary — 14
  References — 14

2 How to Choose a Business School and an MBA Program — 15
  Back to the Roots — 15
  The First European Business Schools — 16
  The First US Business Schools — 16
  The MBA's International Success — 17
  There Is No Typical Business School — 18
  Summary — 32
  References — 32

3 How Accreditations and Rankings Can Guide Your MBA Choice — 37
Summary — 50
References — 51

4 What a Business School Looks for in an MBA Applicant — 53
MBA Admission Patterns — 53
Eight Key Features — 54
Summary — 63
References — 63

5 How Do You Apply for Your Ideal MBA Program — 65
Eight Steps to Lift-Off — 65
Summary — 76
References — 76

Part II Making the Most of Your MBA Studies

6 How to Extract Most Academic Value from Your Business School and MBA Program — 81
The MBA as a Jet Engine — 81
Introduction to Eight Academic Areas — 82
Grades: A Non-issue — 94
Summary — 95
References — 96

7 How to Benefit Beyond the Academic Value of Your Business School and MBA Program — 97
Introduction to Eight Non-academic Areas — 97
Summary — 107
References — 107

Part III Benefiting from the Long-Term Value of Your MBA

8 How an MBA Can Boost Your Career — 111
  Summary — 123
  References — 124

9 How to Get Value from Your MBA Alumni Network — 127
  Lifelong Linkages — 127
  University Alumni Networks — 128
  Alumni Network Rankings — 129
  Friends with Benefits — 131
  Summary — 138
  References — 138

10 Why You Should Already Think About the Long-term Impact of Your MBA Degree — 141
  Thinking About the Future Informs Your Choices — 141
  Strive for an Ikigai Future — 141
  Summary — 150
  References — 151

Appendix A: Financial Times Global MBA Ranking — 157

Appendix B: Financial Times Global Executive MBA Ranking — 161

Appendix C: Triple Crown Accredited Business Schools — 165

About the Authors

Bodo B. Schlegelmilch is the Chair of the Association of MBAs [AMBA] and Business Graduates Association [BGA] as well as a Professor of Management and Strategic Marketing at WU Vienna (Austria). He served as Founding Dean of the WU Executive Academy, the leading business school in Austria, and launched a number of MBA programs, including the Vienna Executive MBA, which he led into the global Financial Times Top 50 ranking.

Bodo chaired MBA peer review accreditation visits across Europe, China, Latin America, and the Asia-Pacific region. He taught in over 30 countries spanning six continents and has received Fellowships from the Academy of International Business, the Academy of Marketing Science, and the Chartered Institute of Marketing in recognition of his teaching and research. The American Marketing Association honored him with the Significant Contribution to Global Marketing Award and the Lifetime Achievement Award for Higher Education, while the Academy of Marketing Science bestowed upon him the Outstanding Marketer of the Year Award. Thammasat University awarded him a Bualuang ASEAN Chair Professorship. Bodo actively serves on advisory boards of European and Asian universities and holds guest professorships in China, Fiji, Thailand, the UK, and the USA.

Bodo co-authored his first book on MBAs more than three decades ago, when he taught at the University of California, Berkeley. More recently, he received the *Journal of Marketing Education's* 2020 Outstanding Article of the Year award for a paper advocating the need for radical innovation of business schools. Bodo has delivered keynote addresses on the future of management education at the Association of Asia-Pacific Business Schools (AAPBS), the Association of American Colleges & Universities (AAC&U), the Association of Indian Management Schools (AIMS), the Chilean Association of Business Schools (ENEFA), the American Marketing Association (AMA), and many others.

Initially educated in Germany, Bodo received two doctorates from the University of Manchester (UK) and an honorary Ph.D. from Thammasat University (Thailand). Starting at Deutsche Bank and Procter & Gamble in Germany, he continued his career at the University of Edinburgh and the University of California, Berkeley. Appointments as British Rail Chair of Marketing at the University of Wales (UK) and Professor of International Business at Thunderbird School of Global Management (USA) followed.

George D. Iliev is Accreditation Director and Director of Strategic Projects & Innovation at AMBA & BGA (the global MBA-accrediting body, headquartered in London). Over a decade, he has been responsible for managing the MBA accreditation of 140 of the leading business schools in Europe, Asia, and America. During his 12 years at AMBA & BGA, he has participated in 200 MBA accreditation visits on all six continents and has reviewed for accreditation/re-accreditation around 1000 MBA programs. At the strategic level, George also focuses on developing initiatives in EdTech, online and executive education, and entrepreneurship education.

Before joining AMBA & BGA in 2011, George had a consulting career touching on media (CNN-Atlanta), sustainability (Bolivia), and renewable energy (Bulgaria); he did macroeconomic research for the Economic Policy Institute; and had a stint of four years as managing editor of a China business news service for Reuters Business Briefing and Dow Jones Factiva. He taught China Business and Economy at Sofia University (2004–2007) and has a professional interest in Entrepreneurship and Innovation research.

George completed his first MBA (2.5 years, part-time) at Sofia University in 2005, when he had barely four years of work experience. In 2010, he completed his second MBA (two years, full-time) at Emory University (Atlanta), where he was a Fulbright Scholar. His Emory MBA included an exchange semester at the Hong Kong University of Science and Technology. George also holds an MSc degree in Economic History and Anthropology from the London School of Economics (where he was a Chevening Scholar) and a Bachelor in Chinese Studies from Sofia University.

George speaks Mandarin Chinese, English, and Spanish, in addition to his native Bulgarian. In his spare time, he writes a blog exploring the parallels between nature and business, under the pseudonym George Eliot (Iliev in Bulgarian).

John A. Quelch served as Senior Associate Dean at Harvard Business School and has been Dean at three leading business schools on three continents, the University of Miami, London Business School, and the China Europe International Business School.

Part I

Finding and Applying for the Right MBA

1

Why Would You Want an MBA

Check Your Rationale

There are good reasons and bad reasons for wanting an MBA. The bad reasons are frequently associated with two negative interpretations of the acronym MBA, namely "**M**ediocre **B**ut **A**rrogant" and "**M**arried **B**ut **A**vailable." If your only reason for obtaining an MBA is to decorate your business card with the desired three-letter MBA title, any business school will do. However, what such MBA graduates may bring to the table is indeed often rather mediocre.

Hoping to spice up your private life through finding a new partner in your MBA program should not be the driving force for joining an MBA program either. While group work sometimes stretches into the early hours of the morning and study trips to foreign destinations are a well-recognized fertile ground for forging new partnerships (as the authors' observation can corroborate), the tongue-in-cheek reference to the MBA as "Married But Available" sends the wrong signal.

So what are the good reasons for pursuing an MBA? Fortunately, there are plenty of good reasons and, as we will show in the next chapter, your specific motivation will determine which type of business school best suits your needs. Here are eight (a lucky number in Buddhism and across

Asia) common motivations for starting an MBA program. Some of them are not mutually exclusive:

1. Converting into Management
Your first degree *is not* in business but, for example, in engineering, chemistry, or medicine, and your current job leads you into managing something. Typically, this "something" includes managing people, budgets, projects, or processes (this is the definition of London Business School for recognizing and categorizing the managerial experience of MBA applicants). While managing people, budgets, and projects is commonly understood as "management," managing processes broadens the concept of managerial experience to include, for example, an engineer managing a production process at a chemicals plant or a journalist managing a web page for an online newspaper.

In fact, many MBA programs were originally conceived as conversion courses for engineers and other non-business specialists, who were promoted into management. Being promoted into management is therefore one of the oldest reasons for pursuing an MBA and creates enormous value for functional specialists advancing into management positions. Many engineers, chemists, or medical doctors start their careers in their respective specialties but over time rise through the ranks and find themselves in situations where they have to manage other people, develop and administer budgets, raise funding, or market their products or services—all tasks for which they have never been trained. Faced with the choice to remain "gifted amateurs" and to randomly pick up some of the required knowledge and skills as autodidacts, many wisely choose to pursue an MBA program and become professional managers.

2. Accelerating to Mid- or Top Management
Your first degree *is* in business or a related field, such as economics or accounting, and you find yourself working in a specific functional area, for example, finance, marketing, or IT. However, your desire is to advance up the hierarchy, which typically requires a broader understanding of general management and an interdisciplinary perspective.

Many undergraduate business, economics, accounting, or finance degrees are relatively theoretical and specialized, and teach little about managing something in "the real world." In contrast, the balance between a theoretical perspective and practical applications shifts more towards practice in MBA programs. That said, MBA programs are not—and in our view should not—be free of theory. As has been pointed out before, there is nothing as practical as a good theory. To this end, an MBA program will teach you useful theoretical perspectives and frameworks and demonstrate how they are applied in management. Another important difference to most undergraduate business courses is the emphasis on skill development that can substantially improve the effectiveness and efficiency of MBA graduates.

3. Changing Careers

You are working in an industry or function that you no longer find interesting or satisfying, but it is hard to leave because you would have to start from square one if you depart too radically from your "beaten path." The MBA can provide a bridge to another industry, especially if the program is long enough to allow an internship in your chosen area. With the help of an MBA, professionals typically leave lower-value sectors (e.g., manufacturing or print media) and move into high-remuneration jobs in tech or finance. And since the grass is always greener on the other side, people sometimes move between equally attractive positions: for example, a junior investment banker may decide to do an MBA to become a management consultant, and vice versa. However, shifting careers is often difficult or unpredictable. Later, we discuss the notorious "triple jump," the problems arising when trying to change all three at once: industry, function, and location.

4. Refreshing Management Knowledge

You already have a number of years of work experience and feel that you need to update your knowledge. After all, our business environment, largely driven by advances in research and technology, is changing so rapidly that some knowledge acquired years or decades ago may become outdated or obsolete.

This point is easy to argue. Just cast your mind back on technologies, companies, and work practices that did not exist a few years ago: Amazon's Alexa was not widely available until 2015; TikTok arrived in 2016; and even Tinder is barely 10 years old. What implications does this have on the marketing of fast-moving consumer companies? Consider the phenomenal growth in home-office work, which was substantially accelerated during the COVID pandemic. How has this changed HR-policies and practices? And what about changes in manufacturing technologies, such as 3D printing? What are the implications, for example, for manufacturing, warehousing, or distribution of such products? Wherever we look, we see changes! And like a vortex that pulls everything with increasing speed into its whirl, the speed of technological change is accelerating. Innovations tend to be interconnected and changes in one field usually lead to changes in another field. In an MBA program, you will analyze and discuss the implications and opportunities of recent innovations. In a good MBA program, you will also be encouraged to think about future trends that may change what we do and how we work. Thus, an MBA is definitely a good means to update your knowledge on the challenges and opportunities innovations bring to the business environment and to your own job.

5. Exploring Entrepreneurship

You have one or more promising business ideas and would like to found a commercial start-up or a social enterprise. Unfortunately, your first degree did not prepare you to become an entrepreneur. Establishing a new company requires strategic insights, functional knowledge, and leadership skills, all of which you can acquire in a good MBA program.

The just-discussed "innovation vortex" offers a plethora of opportunities for new start-ups and entrepreneurs. This coincides with the desire of many business schools to demonstrate their positive contribution to society. Consequently, many business schools have invested in "business incubators," "accelerators," and "start-up labs" designed to help students to convert their entrepreneurial ideas into reality. Later in this book, we will look at some examples in detail. At this stage, you should know that the support and facilities business schools offer in this area differ widely. Thus, if your motivation to pursue an MBA is connected to a plan to become an entrepreneur, you need to have a very close look at what different business schools offer to support your plans.

6. Networking for International Success
You are working in a predominantly domestic environment and would like to acquire a global perspective and a stronger international network in order to push for an international remit in your next job.

While we emphasize the international dimension, the networking aspect of MBA programs is, of course, also important in a domestic environment. When teaching in an Executive MBA program in China, one of the authors came across a student who told him that he was enrolled in two EMBA programs at the same time. He did not necessarily plan to finish both programs, but he was keen to develop his network of classmates. While this may be an extreme case, the networking aspect of MBA programs is not to be underestimated. We have come across many MBA participants who founded companies together; offered each other jobs in the companies they worked for; received job offers from fellow alumni; and helped their peers in making important business connections. Moreover, virtually all business schools have alumni associations: platforms through which MBAs stay in touch after graduation. Organizing get-togethers, learning events, or industry-focused discussion rounds, these alumni associations add real value to graduates (we devote an entire chapter to this). Again, how active business schools are and what they offer to their alumni differs, and while life after graduation sometimes seems a distant consideration when pondering which program to pick, the quality of the alumni network is something that should be at the top of your mind.

7. Utilizing a Trough in Time
You just had a baby and your employer grants you and/or your partner a long parental break. Or you just got made redundant by your company

and were given a decent compensation package. Providing you can afford the time, you may utilize the opportunity to extend your managerial knowledge through a suitable MBA program. This type of opportunity is particularly valuable during an economic recession when finding a lucrative job is more difficult. Many ambitious young executives (especially those working in finance) time their MBA to coincide with a downturn or a financial crisis, as salary bonuses are negligible during hard times.

The potential opportunity arising from a parental break is a tricky case, which strongly depends on the personal circumstances and the family, friends, and support network you can draw on. On the one hand, a sufficiently long parental break offers the opportunity to focus on the next step in your career, and one way of doing this is to invest in an MBA program. On the other hand, your new offspring may simply keep you too busy to devote sufficient time to an MBA program. There are certainly examples showing that attending MBA programs shortly after giving birth can work. We can recall students who were still nursing during their MBA programs. In regular intervals, the partner would visit the school with the baby so that the MBA student could slip out of class to attend to her maternal duties. Of course, this is tough and not everybody wants or can pull this off. That said, there are ample precedents demonstrating that the model can work.

8. Utilizing Company Sponsorship

Your employer recognizes your potential and offers to fund your MBA and/or grant you extra study time. This is often the case in the consulting industry, where doing an MBA is almost considered a "rite of passage" to get promoted from Analyst to Associate or higher.

Such a fortunate situation is akin to winning the lottery. You would be a highly-desired applicant for most business schools, as the fact that your employer is investing in your education suggests you are highly valued and must have performed well in your current job. The fact that you have a guaranteed job after graduation is also something business schools care deeply about, not least because they submit this type of data to the various rankings and post-MBA employment outcomes have a significant weight in the rankings. Of course, there are also cases where employers fund an MBA as part of a redundancy package, but we are focusing on the bright side here. Your employer's sponsorship and support will give you the opportunity to spend precious time on educating yourself and making yourself more valuable on the job market. Thus, there are hardly any reasons why you should not enthusiastically embrace such an offer and embark on an MBA program of your choice.

That said, a company sponsorship comes with some strings attached: typically you would be required to sign an agreement with your employer to continue working for them for two or three years after completing the MBA; or else you would be expected to pay back the funding allocated to you for your MBA tuition. This exit clause is really important as it gives you the freedom to accept a job offer from another company if the overall salary/bonus package on offer is better than your existing salary plus the repayment of the fees.

Explore the Psychographics

Only you will know which of the eight reasons for pursuing an MBA best describes your circumstances. In this context, it is interesting to note that the Graduate Management Admission Council (GMAC): the organization that runs the well-known GMAT test used by many business schools to screen applicants, divides MBA applicants into the following segments: (i) respect seekers, (ii) global strivers, (iii) balanced careerists, (iv) career revitalizers, (v) socio-economic climbers, (vi) skill upgraders, and (vii) impactful innovators.[1] These seven categories overlap with the eight motivations that we have laid out above. You may want to map your rationale for doing an MBA against the psychographic suggested by GMAC and the motivations we discussed and you may even learn something new about yourself from this exercise.

---

[1] GMAC (n.d.).

Fig. 1.1 Ikigai—Japanese concept depicting your Life Purpose or Reason for Being, authors' own figure

Find Your Ikigai

Whether you are working for a big corporation, a small or medium-sized enterprise (SME), a government institution, or a non-governmental organization (NGO), if you are thoughtful, ambitious, and driven, you are probably trying to optimize your "lot" in search of your "Ikigai" (see Fig. 1.1).

Relating the decision to pursue an MBA degree to the Japanese Ikigai concept may sound too grand and too philosophical. However, we believe that the motivation to invest energy, time, and money into an MBA should be well-grounded in your life's purpose. Would it not be ideal if what you love, what you are good at, what the world needs, and what you can get paid for actually overlapped? Thus, considering how an MBA degree can help you find your Ikigai may be less peculiar than it sounds. Essentially, you should try to work out how an MBA could positively contribute to what you want to achieve in life.

Of course, taking such a holistic perspective is not always easy, nor is it obvious. It is not easy because you may not be aware of what you are good at, or even what you like and enjoy. In the course of your MBA, you will invariably improve your self-awareness through diagnostic tests and courses that develop your soft skills. So you may discover that you like finance, for example—a field which you may not have had much to do with before. With their increasing focus on sustainability and corporate social responsibility, MBA programs can also give you insights into what the world needs, in addition to where there are commercial opportunities to get paid more or achieve faster career progression.

Pursuing an MBA allows you to step back and (re)assess what you really want to get out of life. Consequently, it can lead to a completely new orientation in your career. An interesting example we came across in the Vienna Executive MBA is Alexandra. She joined the MBA program with a Ph.D. in Pharmacy. Having spent nearly 20 years in the industry, rising through the ranks to director level with Europe-wide responsibilities at a leading pharmaceutical company, Alexandra used her MBA studies to reassess what she wanted to do in life. After her graduation, she became the General Manager of a leading NGO focusing on food waste and fighting poverty. Most likely this move away from the pharma industry to an NGO reduced her income, but apparently, it increased her happiness. Alexandra loves what she does, she applies her experience and MBA knowledge and excels at her job. She also focuses on something the world needs, and she actually gets paid for doing something good. In short, Alexandra found her true Ikigai.

Embrace the Challenges

Admittedly, most MBA graduates do not join charities or other types of NGOs. Nevertheless, for many MBA graduates, their MBA program has been life-changing. In fact, the Internet is full of blogs in which MBA graduates praise their life-changing MBA experiences.[2] Some business schools even advertise the life-changing potential of their programs. Examples of leading European business schools that tout the life-changing properties of their programs include ESADE[3] in Spain, Aalto[4] in Finland, and Warwick Business School[5] in the UK.

While we recommend using the label "life-changing" carefully, as not all MBA graduates will experience career changes that are as dramatic and fundamental as the one described above, a good MBA program will definitely do more than offer you the latest management insights. A good MBA will challenge you in numerous ways and will transform you as a person. After you complete an MBA, you will have a much better understanding of your strengths, weaknesses, and limitations. Below, we list eight (lucky number again!) challenges that will contribute to your personal development during your MBA:

1. It will challenge you *intellectually* as you will have to learn new material
2. It will challenge your *rhetoric capabilities* as you will have to argue your position in class, for example during case discussions
3. It will challenge your *cultural sensitivity* as you are likely to work with peers who have different cultural backgrounds and values
4. It will challenge your *time management and prioritization* skills as you will need to juggle deadlines for a variety of projects, assignments, and job interviews
5. It will challenge your *leadership skills* as your work in teams and your performance will require you to motivate and organize others
6. It will challenge your *presentation skills* as you will have to present the outcome of your projects in front of your peers, professors, and possibly also senior managers of companies that take part in the so-called live cases
7. It will challenge your *research skills* as you will be tasked to collect and analyse data for a diverse range of projects

---

[2] See, for example, Frankfurt School Blog (2021), Krajcovic (2018), EDHEC Business School (2021).
[3] Esade (n.d.).
[4] Aalto EE (n.d.).
[5] Warwick Business School (n.d.).

8. It will challenge your *writing skills* as you will be required to draft dozens of reports, essays, and executive summaries

Of course, there are other challenges that are not inherent in the content of an MBA program itself but are related to pursuing an MBA. For a start, you need to be aware that an MBA program requires a considerable time commitment, which needs to be balanced against other demands on your time. Most relevant in this context are family and friends and, in case you opt for a part-time MBA program, also your employer, and your ongoing work commitments. It is therefore imperative that your partner (if there is one), your family, and, where applicable, your employer support your studies, as you will inevitably have less time for them during the MBA.

Manage Your Time

The nature of many MBA assignments is that you could always do more. You could spend more time collecting data, more time analyzing a case, more time preparing a presentation, and more time on background reading. And since most MBA students are ambitious, there is a temptation to do just that and neglect family, friends, and work. Needless to say, this is not a desired outcome of participating in an MBA program. Unfortunately, there is no general recipe for finding the right balance between your MBA studies and the other demands on your time. You will learn the term "satisficing" in your MBA: "aiming for a merely adequate/satisfactory result, rather than the optimal." What is right for you may not work for someone else. However, a good start to mitigating the potential problem is recognizing that there is not only the danger of being insufficiently committed to your MBA program but also the danger of being overly committed—to the detriment of other important aspects of your life.

Summary

To summarize, here are the key points: First, there are numerous good reasons for starting an MBA program but the decision should not be taken lightly. We encourage you to think holistically in order to assess how an MBA can contribute to your life goals. Second, a good MBA program offers more than management knowledge. It challenges you in multiple ways, gives you an opportunity to get to know your strengths, weaknesses, and limits, and it can become a truly transformational experience. Last, unless you are a social hermit, an MBA is a team effort. Make sure that you can balance your family, work, and social commitments against the requirements of a program.

References

Aalto EE. (n.d.). *Aalto MBA*. Accessed August 5, 2022, from https://www.aaltoee.fi/en/programs/aalto-mba.

EDHEC Business School. (2021). *EDHEC global MBA: The beginning of a life changing experience*. Accessed August 6, 2022, from https://www.edhec.edu/en/news/edhec-global-mba-beginning-life-changing-experience.

Esade. (n.d.*)*. *Full time MBA - FTMBA - Life-changing experience*. Accessed August 5, 2022, from https://www.esade.edu/mba/en/programmes/full-time-mba/why-were-different/life-changing-experience.

Frankfurt School Blog. (2021). *Why my executive MBA was a life-changing experience*. Accessed August 6, 2022, from https://blog.frankfurt-school.de/why-my-executive-mba-was-a-life-changing-experience/.

GMAC. (n.d.) *Global GME candidate segmentation*. Accessed September 4, 2022, from https://www.gmac.com/market-intelligence-and-research/market-research/global-gme-candidate-segmentation.

Krajcovic, J. (2018). *My MBA — A life changing experience*. Accessed August 6, 2022, from https://www.linkedin.com/pulse/my-mba-life-changing-experience-jakub-krajcovic/.

Warwick Business School. (n.d.) MBA courses. Accessed August 5, 2022, from https://www.wbs.ac.uk/courses/mba/.

2

How to Choose a Business School and an MBA Program

Back to the Roots

In this chapter, we demonstrate how heterogeneous business schools are and argue that MBA applicants need to match their strengths and weaknesses, as well as their future development objectives, with the profiles of the business schools they plan to apply for. Below, we start with a brief look at the history of business schools in order to provide some context.

While economics has been a branch of philosophy and law since Ancient Greece (e.g., Plato),[1] it only emerged as a separate academic subject, called political economy, when writers like Adam Smith (the *Wealth of Nations,* 1776)[2] started theorizing about trade relationships between countries. Economics as a discipline can be traced back to Alfred Marshall, who published a book titled "Economics" in 1890. Given the long history of economics, it may appear astonishing that business schools have a longer history than economics departments in universities.[3]

---

[1] Reisman (2021).
[2] Smith (2010).
[3] Brouwer (2012).

© The Author(s), under exclusive license to Springer Nature Switzerland AG 2023
B. B. Schlegelmilch, G. D. Iliev, *The MBA Compass,*
https://doi.org/10.1007/978-3-031-42739-8_2

The First European Business Schools

The *Aula do Comércio* (School of Commerce) was the world's first government-sponsored school that specialized in the teaching of commerce, including accounting. It was established by the Portuguese Board of Trade, the *Junta do Comércio*, in 1759 and closed in 1844.[4] Meanwhile, ESCP Paris, founded in 1819, is regarded as the world's oldest fully-fledged business school in continued existence.[5] This was followed in 1852 by the establishment of two competing business schools in Antwerp (the Rijkshandelshogeschool and the Sint-Ignatius Handelshogeschool),[6] in 1857 by the world's first public business school in Budapest,[7] and in 1868 by the Ca' Foscari University in Venice.[8]

The First US Business Schools

It was not until 1881 that the Wharton School of the University of Pennsylvania was established. It is commonly, but inaccurately, cited as the world's first business school. Until today, Wharton's website describes it as "the world's first collegiate school of business."[9] Note how the modifier "collegiate" shapes the claim to be the historical first (i.e., as a college within a university, rather than as a stand-alone business school)! Next, in 1900, the Tuck School of Business at Dartmouth College was established as the first graduate school of management in the United States. Tuck is particularly important in the history of business schools in that it conferred the first Master of Science degree in Commercial Sciences. In 1908, the first MBA program was established by the Harvard Graduate School of Business Administration, and in 1943, the first Executive MBA (EMBA) was established at the University of Chicago, Booth School of

---

[4] Rodrigues et al. (2004).
[5] ESCP Europe (n.d.).
[6] University of Antwerp (n.d.) and UCSIA (n.d.).
[7] Budapesti Gazdasági Egyetem (n.d.).
[8] Ca' Foscari (n.d.).
[9] The Wharton School (n.d.).

Business.[10] At that time only American universities offered MBAs.[11] Noteworthy is also the establishment of the Thunderbird School of Global Management[12] in 1946, then called the American Institute for Foreign Trade. Thunderbird was the first graduate management school focused exclusively on global business.

The MBA's International Success

It was not until 1950 that the first MBA program outside the United States was launched by the Ivey School of Business, University of Western Ontario, Canada.[13] One year later, the University of Pretoria in South Africa[14] followed. On the Indian subcontinent, the Indian Institute of Social Welfare and Business Management in Kolkata[15] and the Institute of Business Administration at the University of Karachi[16] became the first institutions to offer MBA degrees, in 1953 and 1955, respectively. In 1957, INSEAD in France[17] became the first European business school to award an MBA. In the following decade, a flurry of new business schools and MBA programs were founded, including ESAN University Graduate School of Business in Lima,[18] the first graduate business school founded in Latin America, as well as renowned institutions in the UK, such as Manchester Business School[19] and London Business School,[20] both established in 1965.

---

[10] Schlegelmilch (2020).
[11] Leach (1993).
[12] Thunderbird School of Global Management (n.d.).
[13] Ivey Business School (n.d.).
[14] University of Pretoria (n.d.).
[15] IISWBM (n.d.).
[16] Pakistani.pk (n.d.).
[17] INSEAD (n.d.).
[18] ESAN (n.d.).
[19] Alliance MBS (n.d.).
[20] London Business School (n.d.).

China, finally, witnessed one of the most dynamic developments. Although commercial education existed before the Second World War,[21] its MBA programs have a short history. The first nine MBA programs in China were launched only in 1991[22]; and today there are more than 240 MBA programs in the country.[23] These days, several Chinese business schools rank among the top in the world[24] and the shift from sending students overseas to offering MBAs in China is accelerating.[25]

There Is No Typical Business School

The history of business schools, founded by former Napoleonic soldiers (ESCP Paris), Jesuits (Antwerp), Royal Decree (Ca' Foscari), private individuals (Wharton), merchants and bankers (Budapest), or the Chinese Ministry of Education (authorizing nine Universities to run the first Chinese MBA programs in 1991) already provides a first indication of their diverse nature. In fact, there is no such thing as a *typical* business school!

According to AACSB, there are more than 16,000 institutions granting business degrees in the world.[26] While not all of them offer MBAs, some institutions offer multiple MBA programs. In India alone, the estimate is for over 3000 business schools; there are no exact numbers. Any attempt to estimate the size of the business school market is further complicated by schools that only offer degrees validated by other degree-awarding institutions. These institutions are often, but not exclusively, based overseas; many Australian, British, Canadian, and New Zealand universities are in the "validation business."[27] Thus, our best estimate—a very rough best estimate—is that there are some 12,000 to 16,000 MBA programs in the world.

---

[21] eChinacities.com (2009).
[22] Lin and Ma (2012).
[23] Sohu.com (2020).
[24] The Financial Times (2021).
[25] Jack (2018).
[26] AACSB (2023).
[27] The Economist (2011).

There is another reason why nobody knows the exact figure. Some programs have an MBA on the box, but not in the box! Would you, for example, count the one-weekend mini-MBAs offered by a company located on top of a butcher's shop as an MBA program? What about programs that liberally grant credits for "life experience?" And what about MBA programs where none of the participants has an undergraduate degree? As someone who looks for a suitable MBA program that fits your needs, you first and foremost have to make sure that you select a program offered by a business school that is credible.

Below, we list eight (lucky number) characteristics that shape business schools and their MBA programs. These eight characteristics are, by no means, a comprehensive taxonomy. However, the criteria we have selected all have a direct impact on the experience you will have during (and possibly also after) the program. Before selecting an MBA program that suits your needs, you should therefore have a good understanding of the differences between business schools and between MBA programs and the consequences these differences may have for different types of MBA applicants. Here are some of the key characteristics that you should consider.

1. Different Sizes of MBA Programs

The number of students in your MBA program will impact your experience. Some of the world's best programs also enroll the largest number of students (Harvard approx. 1600 students; Columbia approx. 1500 students; INSEAD approx. 1000 students; Indian School of Business approx. 800 students). But do not worry: the students do not all sit in one big auditorium, they take their classes in parallel sections. Even so, some boutique programs will provide a more intimate experience for their participants (IEEM in Montevideo, Uruguay <50 students; IEDC-Bled School of Management, in Bled, Slovenia <50 students). Clearly, the degree of personalized care and attention to the individual student tends to be higher in a school with a small MBA class size.

That said, there are a number of advantages to joining larger programs. For a start, there are more networking opportunities, which may help you when looking for business partnerships or facilitate your job search. Moreover, larger programs usually offer more elective options after the core courses that are taken by all participants. From the vantage point of a participant, these permit pursuing a more fine-grained specialization towards the end of an MBA program. Another potential advantage is the greater heterogeneity in backgrounds and opinions of participants, which usually enriches case discussions and project work. In fact, one of the AMBA accreditation criteria requires a minimum MBA intake of at least 20 students taught as a distinct learning group in order to promote mutual learning, peer-to-peer interaction, and diversity. There may also be more choices as far as study trips are concerned and a wider variety of faculty available for supervising student projects and MBA theses/final projects (where applicable—not all MBA programs require a thesis/final project).

As to the latter, an important indicator applicants should look at is the faculty–student ratio. With a faculty–student ratio of around 20 percent, i.e., 1 faculty member for every 5 MBA students, your opportunity for one-to-one time with a faculty member is obviously quite good. However, the faculty–student ratio differs widely.[28] Where MBA programs are embedded into a larger business school or university, the faculty–student ratio of the institution may be relevant, if faculty members who do not teach in the MBA program nevertheless supervise projects.

2. Different Degrees of Internationalization and Diversity

We argue that an international orientation helps to widen the perspectives of MBAs by developing cultural sensitivity, an appreciation of different organizational systems and values, and a better understanding of the opportunities and challenges managers face in different social, economic, legal, and technological environments. Business schools have different options to support the development of an international orientation among their MBA students. The most obvious is the mix of nationalities in the student body. The Financial Times MBA rankings, for example, report the percentage of international students, which can range from 100% for international programs like those of ESCP Business School with campuses in different European countries to 0% for the Indian

---

[28] MBA Guide (2021).

Institute of Management in Bangalore.[29] Other internationalization metrics include the number of international faculty, the international course experience, which focuses on international exchanges and internships, as well as, occasionally, foreign language requirements. Some business schools also require their MBA students to participate in international projects with MBAs from business schools located in other countries. Typical projects, many in collaborations with companies, include market entry projects, the development of business plans, or the drafting of new marketing campaigns. Student teams from different MBA programs can collaborate via video conferencing and other collaboration tools without leaving their home base.

An indication of the degree of internationalization of business schools is the partnerships in which the schools are involved. "The company you keep" is always a helpful rule of thumb: the most prestigious international networks include the schools with the leading brands, so these are likely to offer better opportunities for exchange, case competitions, and joint team projects. For example, the Partnership in International Management (PIM)[30] is a "mutual recognition" network of 69 leading business schools that allows students to easily do an exchange semester at a partner school within the club. Other prestigious international networks are CEMS (a consortium of 34 mostly European schools offering the CEMS Master's in International Management); GNAM (Global Network for Advanced Management, 32 schools); and FOME (the Future of Management Education Alliance of 11 schools, focused on improving online delivery in particular). However, it has to be emphasized that these networks are *not* automatically open to MBA students. They are merely signaling how internationally connected a business school is in general.

An important measure distinguishing between MBA programs is also the gender balance. Similar to the proportion of international students, there are fairly large differences in the ratio of male and female participants in MBA programs, many of them rooted in cultural differences. Chinese MBA programs frequently have more female students (e.g.,

---

[29] The Financial Times (2022).
[30] PIM (n.d.).

Tongji 77%), while Indian programs often struggle to recruit female students (e.g., IIM Calcutta 16%).[31] Of course, there are also other diversity measures. In general, we believe that diversity in terms of gender, ethnicity, nationality, age, etc., contributes to a positive learning experience.

3. Different Organizational Settings

Here, we distinguish between business schools that are stand-alone institutions and schools embedded in larger university settings. While stand-alone business schools are often able to react more quickly to environmental changes, such as the demand for new topics (e.g., marketing analytics), business schools that are part of larger multi-disciplinary universities have more opportunities to collaborate with other departments/schools, which would be more difficult to organize for independent schools. Such collaborations could, for example, consist of joint incubator hubs for entrepreneurial students set up with engineering or IT departments, or collaboration with Law Schools or Medical Schools. Some universities also offer joint-degree programs, such as the JD/MBA in law and business of the University of Chicago Booth Business School and the University of Chicago Law School,[32] or the joint MBA/MD degree offered by the Yale School of Management and the Yale School of Medicine.[33]

Business schools around the world also differ in terms of ownership (public or private) but this is largely a country-wide feature that is determined by how business education in the country evolved historically. For example, in France and Spain, the leading schools are private: in France, they were primarily set up by the chambers of commerce of the respective city (HEC-Paris, ESCP, EMLYON, Kedge, etc.), while in Spain, they were founded primarily by religious institutions (IESE—by Opus Dei; ESADE—by the Jesuits, etc.). On the other hand, in the UK, all top business schools are part of public universities (including LBS, Imperial, Cambridge, Oxford). In the USA, nearly all top business schools are

---

[31] The Financial Times (2022).
[32] The University of Chicago Booth School of Business (n.d.).
[33] Yale School of Management (n.d.).

private: all Ivy League schools, Stanford, Kellogg (Northwestern), Booth (Chicago); but there are also some leading public (state) schools: Berkeley, UCLA, Georgia Tech.

In the top echelons, the ownership of the institution does not make much of a difference for the quality of the MBA. However, in the mid-tiers and lower, it really matters whether the school is for-profit or not-for-profit. All leading business schools worldwide (including all private and public ones listed above) are not-for-profit, which means any surpluses they generate are reinvested within the school or the wider university. Private for-profit institutions are typically lower-tier institutions that invest a lot in marketing and recruiting. Thus, be particularly careful before you engage with such institutions, as they sometimes over-promise and under-deliver, leading to disappointed customers.

In the business school world, not-for-profit institutions that lack snazzy marketing are jokingly described as "not selling what they do"; whereas for-profit institutions are known to "sell what they don't do."

4. Different Focus Areas

The MBA is by design a generalist program with a similar set of core courses. AMBA, for example, requires coverage of 13 subject areas to make a program eligible for AMBA accreditation. Much of the distinctiveness of a program comes from the specializations attached to the program and the way business schools and their MBA programs tend to position themselves. The Babson College in Boston, for example, is well known for its emphasis and expertise in entrepreneurship,[34] INSEAD and London Business School are preferred choices for MBA students who strive for a career in consulting, London Business School and Wharton are well-known for finance and in particular investment banking, while Kellogg at Northwestern continues to have a strong name in marketing. Still, all these programs have a general management orientation despite the concentration on career outcomes for their graduates.

There are also MBA programs that signal their specialization in the title. Typical examples of functionally specialized programs are MBAs in

---

[34] Babson College (n.d.).

Finance, MBAs in Marketing, or MBAs in Entrepreneurship. There are also industry-specialized programs, e.g., the MBA in Healthcare Management of the UCL School of Global Health in London or the Aerospace MBA of Toulouse Business School (based near the headquarters of European plane maker Airbus). Broadly speaking, a *generalist* MBA teaches management knowledge that is applicable in any industry by focusing roughly evenly on all subject areas, while specialized MBAs, sometimes also termed Professional MBAs, focus on the development of management skills in a specific discipline, for example, finance, or a specific industry, for example, healthcare (even though they also provide a generalist management foundation that touches on most/all relevant subject areas). As long as such specialized MBAs maintain a sufficient general management perspective, the Association of MBAs (AMBA) can, in principle, accredit such MBAs. However, if the specialization is too focused on a particular function or industry, AMBA would argue that the program is not an MBA but rather a specialized MSc, as the latter are typically narrower and more focused. Thus, if you really seek a (general!) MBA, you should make sure to check that your chosen program is not over-specialized.

5. Different Program Formats

MBA programs can be categorized according to their delivery format into full-time MBAs, part-time MBAs, online MBAs, and blended MBAs. Full-time MBAs require regular attendance of the program, usually during the day on workdays, which makes it almost impossible to pursue a full-time job at the same time. In the US, full-time MBAs are often two-year programs targeting students who have recently completed their undergraduate degree and who may have some business experience or none at all. Some second-tier universities, again primarily in the US, also offer the so-called 4 + 1 programs. Typically, some business-related undergraduate coursework will be recognized in a subsequent MBA program, which continues with graduate-level courses to fulfill the rest of the MBA requirements.[35] Because of the lack of business experience and the fact

---

[35] Bestaccreditedcolleges.org (2021).

that some subjects are not taught at graduate level, AMBA does not accredit such programs. In Europe, full-time MBAs tend to be one-year programs and typically admit students who have a few years of work experience. One-year MBA programs have also been gaining popularity among the leading US business schools in recent years.[36]

Applicants who want to change careers (industry or function) or change location typically choose a full-time MBA.[37] A big advantage of a full-time MBA may be the opportunity to do an internship as part of or during the program, as well as to do an exchange semester abroad or a shorter overseas stint. In two-year MBAs in the USA, the internship comes in the summer between Year 1 and Year 2. In shorter one-year full-time programs, an internship may follow at the end of the academic courses or be substituted by a consultancy project for a real company. Successful internships often lead to a full-time job offer, which makes career change so much easier.

Part-time MBAs come in all shapes and forms and typically permit participants to pursue a full-time job while studying for an MBA. This may mean studying a few days a week in the evenings, studying Thursday, Friday, Saturday, and Sunday (taking holidays or getting a leave-of-absence for the workdays from the employer, who supports the MBA studies of the employee), or studying in longer blocks (e.g., a week every two months), again covering the MBA time by taking holidays or getting a leave-of-absence from a supportive employer. From the vantage point of a participant, part-time MBA formats tend to offer an ideal way to combine a full-time job with an MBA. However, balancing work commitments with the demands of an MBA program is not easy, in particular as family and personal commitments also demand time. Moreover, some of the part-time formats can stretch over a long period (typically two to three years, although the typical duration of a part-time MBA has been shrinking in recent decades to around 18–24 months)—which in itself requires quite a lot of willpower and determination.

More experienced people (in their 30 s or early 40 s) who want to or need to keep working while doing the MBA typically prefer part-time

---

[36] Mitchell (2021).
[37] Byrne (2019).

MBAs. If you have a family, children, and a mortgage, it is harder to give up your salary and pursue full-time study. When you are close to the mid-point of your career, stopping work would also mean a high opportunity cost (foregone income): a 26-year-old typically earns a lower salary than a 35-year-old does, so it is easier for a younger person to give up their employment and do a full-time MBA.

Modular programs (which are typically branded Executive MBAs/EMBAs) often tend to be preferred by senior executives because they allow the participant to leave behind their work and family obligations and dedicate several days to their studies. Avoiding the need for multi-tasking improves the work–life–family balance. Modular programs also attract a geographically diverse group of participants who often fly in for their module, sometimes even from another continent. For example, the EMBA-Global delivered jointly by LBS and Columbia is composed of modules that rotate between London and New York.[38]

The Association of MBAs (AMBA) has some useful guidelines on what constitutes a genuine EMBA.[39] Typically these are delivered in a modular format to participants who have "over eight years of managerial experience and often have over 12-15 years of total work experience, with incremental and demonstrable levels of seniority in their career in the corporate, entrepreneurial, public or non-profit sectors." However, we advise to always carefully look at the profile of the past participants before selecting an EMBA program. Not every program with the label EMBA is a "genuine" EMBA. Also, be careful with the label "global." This does not automatically mean a more global orientation of the program or a more international group of participants. In this context, an interesting side note. In Japan, the Nagoya University of Commerce and Business (NUCB) registered the term "Global MBA" as a trademark,[40] with the consequence that other Japanese business schools can, at best, call their programs "International MBA."

The programs that have changed the most in recent years are the online MBAs. A decade or two ago, online MBAs were the poor cousin of the

---

[38] EMBA-Global (n.d.).
[39] Association of MBAs (2021).
[40] Japanese Patent Office (n.d.).

on-campus MBA. The recorded videos they used in the distant past were jokingly referred to as "talking heads" (a professor who is talking to the camera for an hour). However, nowadays online MBAs are much more interactive, with a mix of synchronous interaction (real-time, live) and asynchronous (recorded) activities, discussion boards, and gamification elements. A synchronous delivery is a live delivery, i.e., all participants need to log in at the same time as the lecturer and there are elements that require real-time online interactions (e.g., case discussions). In an asynchronous mode, participants are typically given access to online learning materials that are not delivered live, such as recorded video lectures. Most of the recorded videos now contain infographics and cartoons and typically do not exceed 15–18 minutes (the length of a TED talk). They may also need to participate in discussion forums or post on blogs asynchronously (within a certain time period). None of this is happening in real-time and, consequently, participants have more flexibility in deciding when they can devote time to their MBA studies. Online MBAs in the past used to be preferred by people living in remote locations. However, nowadays anyone with a busy life and career can opt for an online MBA, as it allows significant flexibility.

Online MBAs do not require physical presence at a business school, but the lack of personal direct interaction with other participants may also be a substantial disadvantage, as it restricts peer-to-peer learning and may dampen the motivation to stick with the program. In fact, purely online asynchronous programs are known for their low completion rate and AMBA does not accredit online programs with less than 120 synchronously-delivered contact hours. Consequently, most good-quality online MBA programs mix synchronous and asynchronous teaching. In fact, some online programs even involve personal touchpoints, where the participants are required to attend a physical meeting for a few days in the beginning, during, or at the very end of the program.

Blended MBA programs, sometimes also known as hybrid, combine online elements and physical in-person attendance as part of the design of the program rather than at the discretion of the student. Before the COVID pandemic, blended and hybrid were used as synonyms. However, during the pandemic, hybrid started being used primarily to describe a mixed delivery mode in which some students choose to take a class online while others choose to attend the same class in person. On the other hand, blended delivery has always meant a program design with sequential mixing of the two modes: e.g., online delivery for several weeks followed by an on-campus module for all students on a weekend. The term is ill-defined, so you should definitely check out the specific details if an MBA program is advertised as hybrid to make sure that it meets your scheduling constraints. Long-standing examples of blended MBA programs are those delivered by The Open University and by Henley Business School (both based in the UK) for several decades, which combine online study periods followed by on-site modules. In Henley's case, these physical modules are delivered at several hubs around the world.

Accelerated by the COVID pandemic, online and blended MBA programs have grown in size and gained in popularity. Technological advances have made video conferencing and the delivery of teaching material over the Internet widely accessible. In future, we anticipate that other means of delivery, such as via holograms, virtual reality (VR), or the metaverse will result in radical changes in the way MBA programs are offered.[41]

6. Different Faculty Quality and Mix

The quality of the faculty remains the core asset of every MBA program, and this is independent of the delivery method or any other factor that impacts the overall learning experience. Essentially, faculty members need to be knowledgeable, enthusiastic, and pedagogically competent to ensure a positive learning experience and the achievement of the desired learning outcomes. One way of classifying faculty is their engagement in academia (full-time versus part-time academics), their practical experience (e.g., corporate leaders versus pure academics), their academic background (e.g., Ph.D. versus Master's Degree) and their research/teaching focus (teaching-only faculty, research-only faculty, or a mix of teaching and research workload, which is the most common at the leading universities/business schools). Of course, not all of these categories are mutually exclusive, as demonstrated by former corporate leaders with a PhD who turn into full-time academics, or research-active pure academics who

---

[41] Schlegelmilch (2020).

work for a university but regularly engage in corporate consulting. Why is this relevant for MBA students? We believe that good MBA programs should be able to offer a balance between theories and frameworks, on the one hand, and practical insights and examples, on the other hand. It is not helpful for students if the MBA faculty consists only of academics who have never seen a company from the inside and never had the opportunity to gain corporate leadership experience. Equally, it is not helpful if the entire MBA-teaching faculty consists of managers who tell their corporate "war stories" but have no regard for the need to generalize and conceptualize by applying empirically-verified theories and analytical frameworks. As in so many areas of life, it is the right mix that is important.

7. Different Pedagogical Approaches

MBA programs are widely associated with case teaching. Good teaching cases provide narratives about real companies, organizations, or situations in which individuals or groups need to make decisions. Case teaching offers a powerful tool to bring real-world experience into the classroom, positively influences student engagement, and engenders action learning. Consequently, some business schools, for example, Harvard Business School in the US, Nagoya University of Commerce and Business in Japan, or INSEAD in France/Singapore/Abu Dhabi, use the case method as their main mode of instruction. However, even business schools that center their pedagogy on the case method augment pure case teaching with technical notes, background papers, and experiential and immersion fieldwork.

Business simulations, many of which are online, are also a standard staple of business schools. They provide interactive learning experiences which often put students in the role of decision-makers who have to choose between various policy options or strategies (e.g., deciding on a company's marketing mix) and then allow them to trace the impact of their decisions (e.g., the achieved market share or profitability). As many of these simulations are competitive, they greatly enhance student engagement. The so-called live-cases, student consulting projects, or corporate-led business competitions in which teams from different business schools compete are also frequent pedagogical tools used in MBA programs.

Of course, standard lectures are also used in MBA teaching. However, even within lectures, good MBA instructors include discussion to enhance student engagement and to give students opportunities to hone their speaking and argumentation skills. In this context, MBA programs also typically include multiple assignments, in which students have to present their analyses and defend their arguments in front of their classmates. Taken collectively, good MBA programs tend to focus on student-centered learning approaches that foster student interaction and engagement and, in the process, also improve their rhetorical, debating, and presentation skills.

8. Different Peer Groups, Alumni, and Placement Support

An important characteristic of MBA programs is peer-to-peer learning. To this end, you should carefully review the background of the previous intakes of students who have attended the MBA programs that you are considering. Do they have sufficient managerial expertise to serve as a worthy source of learning for you? Do they come from functions or industries you are particularly interested in? Is the program attracting entrepreneurs you can relate to? Would you be comfortable with the average age, range of nationalities, and gender mix?

It also does not harm to scrutinize the composition of the MBA alumni. Look at the career patterns of the MBA graduates: in which industries, countries, and positions do they work? Is the alumni association well-organized? What kind of meetings and events do they offer? Some alumni organizations, for example, have active subgroups focusing on particular industries. Also, ask how the business school supports alumni activities.

Depending on your personal career plans, you may want to use the MBA to find a new job. If this is the case, you should look into the job-placement support that the business school offers. Good schools will have designated career centers that may help you draft your application package, including your resume/curriculum vitae (CV) and cover letters, provide interview training, organize meetings with potential employers, set up CEO lunches, and arrange connections to professional recruiters and head-hunters. Beware that the support needed by mid-career MBAs is rather different from what fresh university graduates need when looking for their first job, and this should be clearly reflected in the career support. Some MBA programs embedded in larger universities try to point their MBA graduates to their general career center, which is primarily geared towards placing young graduates in their first job. In such an arrangement, mid-career MBAs need to be particularly wary (and vocal) to ensure that they receive adequate support.

Before you apply to a business school, a quick look at the composition of the school's board of trustees, advisory board, and alumni board will give you a good helicopter view of the school's biggest success stories. It would be a great mark of quality if you can recognize these people and/or find them impressive. You may also want to factor in the overall university alumni network, in addition to the alumni of the MBA programs and the business school. The alumni networks of many leading universities such as Oxford, Cambridge, and Harvard are seen as equally or even more prestigious than the alumni networks of their business schools (the latter forming a subset of the former). In a minority of cases, however, the business school is the only one that really matters. For example, London Business School has one of the most prestigious alumni networks anywhere in the world, while the university technically belongs to the University of London, a loose confederation of London-based universities that includes a variety of institutions that compete in less prestigious market segments (e.g., Birkbeck).

Some business schools integrate the online platform UniBuddy in their admissions process to help set up conversations between prospective and current students. However, this connection is made via an admissions officer, so you need to have started an official conversation with the school to benefit from the UniBuddy platform functionality. And even if a school does not have automated matching of candidates to students, you can still request the admissions officer to connect you to a current MBA student for a chat—though this is usually done after you have applied.

Schools that are proud of their alumni's achievements will collect and post statistics about their career progression. Schools that do not flaunt their alumni are either not particularly proud of them, or not even aware of what their alumni are up to. If you can see career/alumni statistics on the school's website, that is a positive sign for the quality of the alumni network.

Many of the characteristics discussed are also scrutinized by accreditation agencies such as AMBA, AACSB, and EFMD. Different MBA program rankings, such as those compiled by the Financial Times, QS, or US News and World Report, also compare and emphasize different alumni, job-placement, and career-related criteria. Consequently, you should also seek a good understanding of the role and value of accreditations and rankings. In Chap. 3, we will focus on how you may use accreditations and rankings in finding an MBA program that fits your needs.

Summary

To summarize, here are the key points: First, business schools initially emerged in Europe before becoming the hallmark of US management education. From the US, business schools and MBA programs expanded into other parts of the world. Most recently, China has witnessed a formidable boom in MBA programs. Second, given the long and diverse history of business schools, many different formats and variants have emerged. Consequently, there is no such thing as a typical business school. Third, potential MBA applicants need to be aware of the key differences between programs and how these may impact their learning experience and their desired career trajectories.

References

AACSB. (2023, May 1). Worldwide business schools estimate of 16,565 institutions – by Robert Colin Nelson. *AACSB Senior Manager of Data Analysis*.

Alliance MBS. (n.d.) *Homepage*. Accessed August 13, 2022, from https://www.alliancembs.manchester.ac.uk/.

Association of MBAs. (2021). *EMBA definition (Guidelines)*. Accessed April 15, 2023, from https://www.associationofmbas.com/app/uploads/2021/01/EMBA-Definition.pdf.

Babson College. (n.d.) *Full time MBA*. Accessed August 19, 2022, from https://www.babson.edu/graduate/academics/full-time-business-programs/mba/.

Bestaccreditedcolleges.org. (2021, October 20). 4+1 MBA programs. *Bestaccreditedcolleges*. Accessed August 20, 2022, from https://bestaccreditedcolleges.org/articles/4-1-mba-programs.html.

Brouwer, M. (2012). *Organizations, individualism and economic theory*. Routledge.

Budapesti Gazdasági Egyetem. (n.d.) *History*. Accessed August 13, 2022, from https://web.archive.org/web/20161128201421/http:/en.bgf.hu/About-Us/history.

Byrne, A. J. (2019, April 2). Why the MBA is the right choice for career switchers. *Poets & Quants*. Accessed April 15, 2023, from https://poetsandquants.com/2019/10/02/mba-for-career-switchers/.

Ca' Foscari. (n.d.) *About us*. Accessed August 13, 2022, from https://www.unive.it/pag/24289/.

eChinacities.com. (2009, September 25). China's 20 oldest universities. *eChinacities*. Accessed August 12, 2022, from https://www.echinacities.com/china-media/Chinas-20-Oldest-Universities.

EMBA-GLOBAL. (n.d.) *Overview*. Accessed April 15, 2023, from https://www.emba-global.com/overview.

ESAN. (n.d.) *About Esan*. Accessed August 13, 2022, from https://www.esan.edu.pe/en/about-esan.

ESCP Europe. (n.d.) *The world's first business school*. Accessed August 12, 2022, from http://www.escpeurope.eu/escp-europe/history-of-escp-europe-business school.

IISWBM. (n.d.) *Homepage*. Accessed August 13, 2022, from https://www.iiswbm.edu/.

INSEAD. (n.d.) *Homepage*. Accessed August 13, 2022, from https://www.insead.edu/.

Ivey Business School. (n.d.) *IVEY Business School*. Accessed August 13, 2022, from https://www.ivey.uwo.ca/.

Jack, A. (2018, September 27). China business schools are evolving rapidly. *The Financial Times*. Accessed August 13, 2022, from https://www.ft.com/content/0ad44c16-bdbc-11e8-8dfd-2f1cbc7ee27c.

Japanese Patent Office. (n.d.) *Trademark inquiry*. Accessed June 19, 2023, from https://www.j-platpat.inpit.go.jp/c1800/TR/JP-2009-012043/396DF6463BC19BDE9BE17AF514072FB63923A1409176C582-E973F0DAA47DFB4F/40/en.

Leach, W. (1993). *Land of desire: Merchants, power, and the rise of a new American culture*. Pantheon Books.

Lin, J., & Ma, H. (2012). Research on internationalization and the localization of China's MBA education. *World Journal of Education, 2*(6), 20–23.

London Business School. (n.d.) *Homepage*. Accessed August 13, 2022, from https://www.london.edu/.

MBA Guide. (2021). 100 best MBA programs ranked by student/faculty ratio. *MBA Guide*. Accessed August 18, 2022, from https://www.mbaguide.org/mba-programs-ranked-student-faculty-ratio/#mba-programs-ranked-by-student-faculty-ratio.

Mitchell, B. (2021, August 6). The rise of the one-year MBA. *Poets & Quants*. Accessed April 12, 2023, from https://poetsandquants.com/2021/08/06/the-rise-of-the-accelerated-one-year-mba/.

Pakistani.pk. (n.d.) Institute of Business Administration, Karachi. *Pakistani*. Accessed August 13, 2022, from https://pakistani.pk/institute-of-business-administration-karachi/.

PIM. (n.d.) *Member schools*. Accessed April 17, 2023, from https://pimnetwork.org/pim-schools/.

Reisman, D. (2021). *Plato's economics: Republic and control*. Edward Elgar Publishing.

Rodrigues, L. L., Gomes, D., & Craig, R. (2004). The Portuguese School of Commerce, 1759–1844: A reflection of the enlightenment. *Accounting History, 9*(3), 53–71.

Schlegelmilch, B. B. (2020). Why business schools need radical innovations: Drivers and development trajectories. *Journal of Marketing Education, 42*(2), 93–107.

Smith, A. (2010). *The wealth of nations: An inquiry into the nature and causes of the wealth of nations*. Harriman House Limited.

Sohu.com. (2020, May 28). List of 246 MBA education institutions in China. *Sohu*. Accessed April 12, 2023, from https://www.sohu.com/a/398321209_99997057.

The Economist. (2011, October 15). Trouble in the middle: Is time running out for business schools that aren't quite elite?. *The Economist*. Accessed December 20, 2022, from https://www.economist.com/briefing/2011/10/15/trouble-in-the-middle.

The Financial Times. (2021, October 17). EMBA 2021 - Business school rankings. *The Financial Times*. Accessed August 13, 2022, from https://rankings.ft.com/rankings/2863/emba-2021.

The Financial Times. (2022, February 13). *MBA 2022 - Business school rankings*. *The Financial Times*. Accessed August 18, 2022, from https://rankings.ft.com/rankings/2866/mba-2022.

The University of Chicago Booth School of Business. (n.d.) *JD/MBA Joint-Degree Program*. Accessed August 19, 2022, from https://www.chicagobooth.edu/mba/joint-degree/jd-mba?source=ent-se-bi-pd-camp:ppc21-brand-eurfall&term=https%3A%2F%2Fwww.chicagobooth.edu%2Fmba%2Fjoint-degree%2Fjd-mba&msclkid=47c63298ee621853e4e35067be763418&utm_source=bing&utm_medium=cpc&utm_campaign=HPN%20-%20Brand%20-%20London%20-%20Europe&utm_term=https%3A%2F%2Fwww.chicagobooth.edu%2Fmba%2Fjoint-degree%2Fjd-mba&utm_content=HPN%20-%20BrandY0London%20-%20Europe%20-%20dynamic%20ad%20group.

The Wharton School. (n.d.) *The world's first business school*. Accessed August 12, 2022, from https://www.wharton.upenn.edu/about-wharton.

Thunderbird School of Global Management. (n.d.) *About Thunderbird*. Accessed August 13, 2022, from https://thunderbird.asu.edu/about.

University of Antwerp. (n.d.) *History*. Accessed August 22, 2022, from https://www.uantwerpen.be/en/about-uantwerp/organisation/facts-figures-rankings/history/.

University of Pretoria. (n.d.). *Homepage*. Accessed August 13, 2022, from https://www.up.ac.za/.

USCIA. (n.d.) *Who we are*. Accessed August 22, 2022, from https://www.ucsia.org/home-en/organization/who-we-are/.

Yale School of Management. (n.d.) *MBA/MD with Yale School of Medicine*. Accessed August 19, 2022, from https://som.yale.edu/programs/joint-degrees/mba-md-yale-school-medicine#:~:text=MBA%2FMD%20with%20Yale%20School%20of%20Medicine%20The%20joint,with%20managing%20change%20in%20a%20tumultuous%20healthcare%20environment.

3

How Accreditations and Rankings Can Guide Your MBA Choice

Rankings and accreditations can both help you to make important MBA decisions, but there are major distinctions between these two key influencers. First, rankings are primarily quantitative, while accreditations are mostly qualitative. Second, the aggregated data collected by rankings is published or at least deducible from the relative standing of the institution; while the data submitted for an accreditation does not get published (and neither is the accrediting body's final report made public). Ultimately, rankings work on the creation of a rank-ordered list that unwittingly pits every school against the others; while accreditation agencies work on quality control and consultancy-type service for the schools' leadership team that, as a side effect, creates a global network of institutions with the same accreditation. We lay out in eight points below how rankings and accreditations differ and how they can be useful.

1. Rankings at a Glance

Rankings are hugely influential for recruiting MBA participants (and all other types of students) but their role is also notoriously contentious and the factors on which rankings are based are hotly debated. In some ways, rankings resemble the sour British yeast-extract spread Marmite with its marketing slogan: "Love it or hate it." MBA applicants tend to love the simplicity of rankings, as the complexity of the world is boiled down into a simple numbered list. On the other hand, business schools (and their marketing and admissions departments) are a lot more ambivalent about rankings, even if they do well in them. Each additional ranking requires a lot of work in preparing and submitting data and alumni contacts and ultimately investing in targeting improvements in the specific factors that influence the ranking. Furthermore, marketing departments have to deal with the fallout of each new ranking announcement, as statistically half the time the institution will drop in the ranking, and such moves have organizational and political ramifications. Nowadays, the annual performance review of a business school dean may also include their school's performance in key rankings and these rankings can even impact the dean's salary and annual bonus.

For the applicants who have the least amount of information, rankings hold immense importance. However, once you have read our MBA Compass and talked to a few stakeholders, you should realize that rankings are merely a useful heuristic (shortcut) that should be used in conjunction with all the other multiple sources of information and tools to aid your decision-making process.

The leading MBA and business school rankings are published by the Financial Times, U.S. News & World Report, Bloomberg Businessweek, Forbes, and QS. There are also university rankings (e.g., Times Higher Education ranking and the Shanghai Ranking); regional rankings such as America Economia (for Latin America); specialized rankings, e.g., Poets & Quants Top 50 MBAs for Entrepreneurship ranking; and national (country-by-country) rankings such as EdUniversal, which can be useful for students interested in smaller countries and institutions that are not in any of the global rankings. Typically, all these rankings are accessible for free even though the media publications maintain paywalls that require paid subscription for accessing all other articles.

Some rankings existed in the past but have been suspended: The Economist used to publish an influential MBA ranking but discontinued it in 2022; while the Wall Street Journal used to have an MBA ranking but now produces only a US College Ranking in partnership with Times Higher Education.

2. Accreditation at a Glance

Accreditation for business schools is a quality assurance/quality enhancement process: it aims to verify that quality standards are met; and it also aims to help institutions improve beyond their current standing. In the simplest terms, these two aspects of the accreditation process can be described as inspection and consultancy, respectively. The succinct outcome that is announced publicly is typically a decision to accredit/re-accredit the business school for three or five years.

The leading international accreditations in the MBA/business school space are: AMBA by the London-based Association of MBAs (now AMBA & BGA); EQUIS by the Brussels-based European Foundation for Management Development (EFMD); and AACSB by the Florida-based Association to Advance Collegiate Schools of Business. There are also regional accreditations, e.g., FIBAA primarily in the German-speaking world; CEEMAN in Central and Eastern Europe; and CAMEA in China.

The outcome of accreditation visits is not particularly fine-grained for the outside world. AACSB awards five-year accreditations only. The period of AMBA and EQUIS accreditation is three or five years, a three-year accreditation is typically awarded to schools that are given multiple conditions by the peer-review panel and are asked to implement changes and submit progress reports; while a five-year accreditation is awarded to schools whose visit ends without conditions or with minor conditions. A crucial difference between AMBA and EQUIS accreditation is that EQUIS publishes the accreditation period on its website while AMBA does not. There are pros and cons to both approaches: making the period of accreditation public helps prospective students (as well as competitor institutions) gauge the performance of the institution; while not publishing it reduces the tensions during the accreditation visit and contributes to more collaborative and open discussions.

All three accreditation processes involve a review of the institution and of sample programs. However, in an EQUIS or AACSB visit, the sample programs do not have to include the MBA by default (though sometimes the MBA is indeed the sample program). On the other hand, AMBA accreditation always reviews all the MBA programs (and optionally, any MSc Management/MIM or DBA programs). All three bodies also have a range of additional (secondary) accreditations: Accounting accreditation by AACSB, Program accreditation by EFMD, and BGA impact and sustainability accreditation by AMBA & BGA.

3. Factors and Formats of Rankings and Accreditations

Rankings and accreditations differ in the number of factors that are taken into account to assess an institution and the process of review. Rankings require the submission of usually no more than 10–20 types of data. Consequently, rankings are sometimes accused of taking a limited or skewed snapshot of institutions and programs. Rankings are always a desktop exercise but the data is re-submitted every year (or biennially for some rankings, e.g., Forbes), which allows tracking the progress of an institution in a comparable manner across many years. The publishers of the rankings do perform spot checks and data audits to ensure the integrity of the submitted data (the Financial Times outsources this type of checks to auditor KPMG); and statisticians check for anomalies in the data as an additional assurance.

In contrast, an accreditation process balances many more qualitative and quantitative factors. For example, the MBA accreditation criteria of AMBA deal with 160 different aspects of the institution and its portfolio of MBA programs, from work experience and seniority of the students to the functioning of the career center, to the number and type of alumni events held annually. This information is submitted as part of a set of data-heavy Self-Assessment Forms and a descriptive (text-heavy) Self Audit Report several weeks before the accreditation panel visit. Accreditations are conducted by a peer-review panel, which is typically composed of deans and directors from other accredited institutions. The peer-review panel visits the school for 2–3 days to review additional documentation and to have structured conversations with stakeholders at all levels. Because of the scale of this type of exercise, re-accreditation visits only take place every three or five years. Based on all this wealth of inputs, accreditation reports paint a rich picture, but the fact that they are not made public creates a sense of secrecy in the outside world. However, neither schools nor accrediting agencies would want to put out in public so much detail about the inner workings of an institution, as this information could be used by competitors. Thus, the accreditation reports remain primarily a consultancy exercise for the benefit of the dean and the school's leadership team. Only the outcome of the visit is disclosed on the website of the accreditation agency, in the form of a list of schools with accredited status, while the school is awarded the right to start using the "Accredited by …" logo on its website and in marketing materials.

Because of the range of information inputs, the duration of the visit and the depth of discussions, an accreditation process cannot be influenced by the school as easily as a ranking can. We do not mean "influencing" in a nefarious way, but rather in the sense that the school can design a targeted strategy that ticks all the necessary boxes. Many business schools have such "beat the rankings" strategies: where to focus at which point in time and how much to invest in "nailing" each of the key indicators. There is nothing devious in this, but such a strategy can lead to a narrow view of what improvements schools may choose to target. For example, the Financial Times Global MBA ranking allocates 32% weight to the salary of MBA graduates (down from 40% before the 2023 ranking: 16 percentage points for the weighted salary of MBA alumni and 16 percentage points for the salary increase pre/post-MBA).[1] Hence, it is not surprising that many MBA directors who want their program to go up in the ranking actively aim to increase the salary of their MBA graduates. This is a noble goal in itself and, in theory, should be aligned with the interests of the students, but some of the instruments to achieve it can be seen as borderline. For example, discouraging entrepreneurial careers and not admitting entrepreneurially-minded candidates can lead to higher average alumni salaries as the founders of start-ups typically do not make much money in the first years after the launch of their company.

4. Ranking of Rankings and Triple Accreditation

Rankings and accreditations can be useful to applicants in different ways. Accreditation agencies publish lists of their accredited institutions, typically containing several hundred entries, which categorize the world into two groups: the accredited and the non-accredited. On the other hand,

---

[1] Jack et al. (2023).

rankings paint a much more competitive picture that allows an applicant to target the "Top 5" schools or the "Top 30–50" schools.

Many prospective applicants create their own "ranking of rankings" with the laudable idea of minimizing the bias of individual rankings and aggregating the factors. Creating your own ranking also allows you to allocate weights to separate rankings or to individual factors/indicators/criteria that are crucial for you. This works well for the top schools, which are present in all or most rankings. One major factor you may want to allocate weight to in your personal ranking of rankings is location: whether you prefer to study in a global city or "tucked away in a corner" in the countryside (e.g., at Tuck or Cornell—no pun intended).

In accreditation, the overlap between different accreditations even has a name: schools that have all three main international accreditations are called "Triple-Accredited" or "Triple Crown" schools. As shown in the diagram (Fig. 3.1) that we have drawn below, a total of 124 schools have AMBA + AACSB + EQUIS as of mid-2023,[2] of which 26 are in the UK, 19 are in France, and 14 are in China (including Hong Kong and Macau).

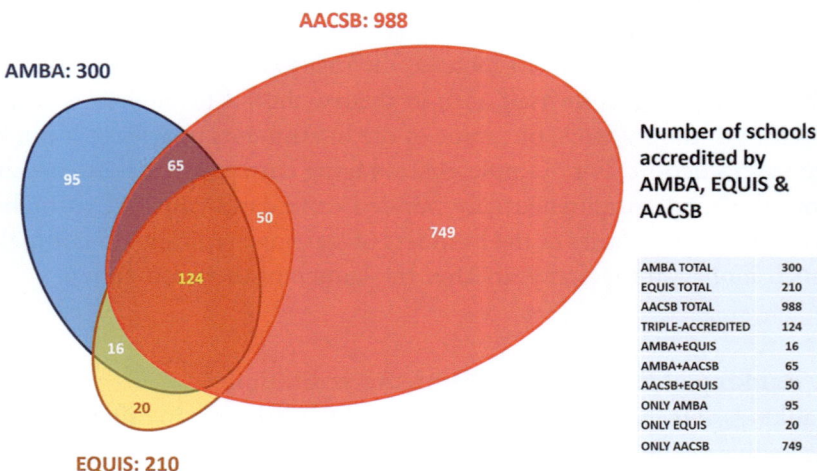

Fig. 3.1 Triple Crown/Triple-Accredited Business Schools, authors' own figure

---

[2] AMBA (n.d.), AACSB (n.d.). and EQUIS (n.d.).

All 124 Triple-Accredited schools are listed by country in an appendix at the end of the book. By and large, institutions that are Triple-Accredited or included in most Top 100 or Top 50 rankings would be considered "safe bets."

5. Particular Aspects of Rankings and Their Rationale

Academic themes have very little input into the rankings. If there is an academic factor involved, it is related to the research of the school's faculty rather than to the academic achievements of the students. Neither the academic success of students before the MBA (e.g., undergraduate GPA or GMAT score) nor academic performance during the MBA matters to the rankings. This is partly because it is difficult to standardize different national grading systems, apart from the GMAT/GRE, which are global and hence perfectly standardized (but then not all schools require them). More importantly, it is because grades matter very little in a student's subsequent career. Milton Friedman famously said that "the business of business is business" and it seems that the business of business school rankings is still mostly business.

Alumni responses often have a significant weight in rankings: for example in the Financial Times rankings, the alumni responses have a weight of 56% in the Global and EMBA rankings and 59% in the Online MBA ranking. Relying on surveys of alumni, students, and (occasionally) employers appears to be a quest for objectivity, but is more subjective than hard data. It can occasionally even be problematic from an ethical/integrity perspective. School staff are not allowed to influence the inputs into the survey but are responsible for providing the list of email addresses of the recipients (without applying any selection to them). Schools that intentionally or unintentionally ignore the rankings' guidance not to communicate with alumni about the survey risk getting delisted from a ranking for a year. Delisting also happens due to lack of participation: if a school's alumni fail to respond to the survey in sufficient numbers, the minimum response ratio for inclusion in the ranking may not be met. For example, the Financial Times requires for the Global MBA ranking a minimum of 20 completed surveys per school and a minimum 20% response rate. Most recently, this happened to Wharton: the school failed to reach this threshold and dropped out of the 2023 Financial Times Global MBA Ranking, after having been ranked No 1 in the world in the 2022 ranking.[3]

There are rankings of Full-Time (also known as Global), Executive, and Online MBA programs. However, there is no ranking of Part-Time MBAs (which is a broader category that includes both the EMBA and evening/weekend MBA programs for junior executives) and of Blended MBA programs (which the Financial Times lumps into the Online MBA ranking if at least 70% of the program is delivered online). The boundary between EMBA and Part-Time MBA programs and between Online and Blended MBAs is blurred and understandably hard to delineate.

University-level, school-level, and program-level rankings are often closely connected, so if you care about rankings, you should pay attention to rankings at all levels. There are at least three reasons for this. First, all degree graduates of all programs, ranked and unranked, will join your institution's alumni network, so 10 years down the line, program boundaries get blurred. Second, the reputational benefits of a university having a leading program or school feed into other programs. Third, expertise in some programs may have a direct effect on the other programs: if a school is a leader in custom Executive Education, this suggests a close relationship with companies. As custom programs are designed for corporate executives and are often delivered on the company's premises, this translates into better employment opportunities and highly qualified professors who are experienced in teaching senior executives.

Some rankings have a different scope but may still be relevant to an MBA applicant. For example, the global ranking/index of think tanks compiled by the University of Pennsylvania names Brazil-based Fundação Getúlio Vargas (FGV) as the leading think tank in Latin America, which suggests that FGV is a school with a very strong research track record.[4]

If you really want to understand the motivation behind the existence of rankings and accreditations, a quick look at how these processes are financed can be quite revealing. In business, this is called "follow the money." Media publications develop rankings for two reasons: to create content for their pages and to attract schools/universities to advertise on

---

[3] Byrne (2023).
[4] University of Pennsylvania (2021).

their pages. The daily edition when a ranking comes out is accompanied by special reports and supplements on business education, which creates opportunities for additional advertising revenue. QS, which is not a media company, has a different business model: it gains visibility through its rankings and thus attracts potential customers for its portfolio of education services, from recruiting support (QS Enrolment Solutions) to QS Ratings (a consultancy service for universities that is distinct from the rankings). On the other hand, accreditation agencies have a much more direct revenue-generating model: they charge flat annual membership fees and fixed peer-review panel visit fees. Advertising in a newspaper or buying recruiting services is not a pre-condition for inclusion in a ranking but paying accreditation fees is a requirement to be considered for accreditation. However, to safeguard the integrity of the accreditation process, the accreditation decision is made by panels of academics from other institutions who are not employees of the accrediting body.

6. Financial Times Rankings Overview

We take a closer look at two sets of rankings: the Financial Times[5] and QS[6] rankings, which are arguably the most influential internationally, while QS has also been the fastest-growing in recent years.

The Financial Times published its first MBA ranking (the Global MBA ranking) in 1999. It included 50 programs worldwide: all of them in America and Europe and none in Asia.[7] Coincidentally, this was also the year when INSEAD opened its Singapore campus (in addition to Fontainebleau, France) and became a dual-center school. The rise of Asia has been spectacular ever since, with Asian schools now taking up 19 places in the 2023 Global MBA ranking (including two for the France/Singapore dual locations of INSEAD and ESSEC); and 32 places in the 2022 EMBA ranking.

The Financial Times publishes seven rankings throughout the year:

---

[5] The Financial Times (2023).
[6] QS University Rankings (n.d.).
[7] Ortmans (2018).

- Global MBA
- Executive MBA
- Online MBA
- Executive Education (Open and Custom)
- MSc Finance (Pre-experience and Post-experience)
- MSc Management
- European Business Schools

The calendar of release of these publications shows a pattern: a new ranking comes out roughly once every two months. This sequence helps manage the workload of the small Financial Times department of statisticians and data gatherers; as well as creates a pipeline of meaningful content that can drive newspaper sales and attract advertising revenue year-round.

The Global MBA ranking is composed of 21 criteria; eight of these criteria are based on alumni responses and have a combined weight of 56%. The EMBA ranking is composed of 15 criteria; five of these criteria are based on alumni responses (current salary, salary increase, career progress, work experience, and aims achieved) with a combined weight of 56% as well. The Online MBA ranking is composed of 20 criteria; nine of the criteria are based on alumni responses with a combined weight of 59%.[8]

As an example, the 21 criteria of the Global MBA ranking with their respective weights in brackets are listed below. They demonstrate the sophistication of rankings design, including the efforts of the Financial Times to keep the rankings relevant and to reflect current trends such as internationalization, gender balance, and sustainability. The last two sustainability-related criteria have been added in the last five years.

- Weighted salary of alumni (16%)
- Alumni salary increase pre-/post-MBA (16%)
- Value for money: tuition fee vs. alumni salary (5%)
- Alumni career progress: promotions since graduation (3%)
- Aims achieved for alumni (4%)

---

[8] The Financial Times (n.d.).

- Alumni network rank (4%)
- Careers service (3%)
- Alumni employed three months after graduation (2%)
- Sector diversity rank before admission (3%)
- Female students (3%)
- Female faculty (3%)
- Women on advisory board (1%)
- International faculty (3%)
- International students (3%)
- International board members (1%)
- International mobility of alumni (5%)
- International course experience during studies (3%)
- Faculty with a doctorate (5%)
- Faculty research rank: publications in 50 journals selected by the FT (10%)
- Carbon footprint rank (4%)
- Environmental, Social and Governance (ESG) and net zero teaching rank: teaching hours on ESG in core courses (3%)

One somewhat random limitation in two of the Financial Times rankings is that the Global and Online MBA rankings only consider programs taught in English (while the EMBA ranking does not have this limitation). In the past, this could have been explained by the requirement for alumni to fill in the survey in English, but with automated translations, this is hardly a relevant constraint anymore. However, since the readership of the Financial Times is primarily English-language based, rankings of English-language MBAs serve an English-language audience better.

7. QS Rankings Overview

QS is the only leading publisher of rankings that is not a media company. The organization first grew in the 1990s with its World MBA Tour (an MBA recruiting fair) and has kept adding marketing and recruiting services in higher education over three decades while also expanding into the university space with institutional and subject rankings. Between 2004 and 2009, QS and Times Higher Education collaborated to produce a joint global university ranking, but since 2009 both have been producing their own rankings separately.

QS is the most prolific rankings engine in the academic space. It churns out the following rankings:

- QS World University Rankings (of 1400 universities: individually ranked from 1 to 600; then in bands of 50 between 600 and 800; and in bands of 200 between 800 and 1400)
- University rankings by region (Asia alone has 760 universities ranked; and Latin America has 428)
- Rankings by Subject (in 51 disciplines, of which Business and Management Studies is one)
- Global MBA Ranking (of 300 business schools with full-time MBA programs: of which 1–100 are individually ranked; 101–150 are ranked in bands of 10; and 151–300 are ranked in bands of 50). These include 115 in the USA, 78 in Europe, 46 in Asia, 22 in Canada, 15 in Oceania (including Australia), 15 in Middle East and Africa, 11 in Latin America
- QS Master's Rankings in Business Analytics; Management; Finance; and International Trade
- Sustainability ranking of 700 universities
- Graduate Employability ranking of 550 universities

The time stamp that QS puts on its rankings is "current year plus one," so the 2024 QS rankings are published in 2023, allowing universities and schools to print their QS rank on marketing materials that stay current for longer. Ironically, some of the data in the "2024" rankings published in 2023 will have been collected in 2022.

The QS Global MBA Rankings uses two surveys (QS Global Employer Survey and QS Global Academic Survey) as well as data submitted by the business schools. The 13 criteria[9] on which the ranking is based (with weights in brackets) are:

---

[9] Top MBA (2022).

3 How Accreditations and Rankings Can Guide Your MBA Choice

- Employability, from QS Global Employer Survey (35%)
- Employment rate three months after graduation (5%)
- Alumni outcomes (10%)
- Entrepreneurship among alumni (5%)
- 10-year return on investment (15%)
- Payback month, i.e., the time it takes to recover the tuition cost, on average 3.5 years (5%)
- Academic reputation (10%)
- Research impact (2.5%)
- Percentage of faculty with Ph.D. (2.5%)
- Female students (2.5%)
- Female faculty (2.5%)
- International students (2.5%)
- International faculty (2.5%)

Comparing the criteria used in the Financial Times and QS Global MBA rankings reveals that the Financial Times ranking is the more data-driven of the two. Surveys are notoriously subjective, but the survey the Financial Times uses asks individual alumni about their personal experience and their own statistics; whereas the QS surveys of employers and academic reputation ask for aggregated data, much of which is purely opinion-based.

8. Other Elite School Groupings

Separately from rankings and accreditations, there are informal (or sometimes even formal) groupings of the leading universities or business schools in a country that can influence the choice of school/MBA. The leading national groupings in five major countries are:

- The informal M7 group in the USA ("the magnificent seven"): Harvard, Stanford, MIT Sloan, Columbia, Wharton (UPenn), Kellogg (Northwestern), Chicago Booth
- Go8 in Australia ("Group of Eight"): Adelaide, Australian National, Melbourne, Monash, UNSW, Queensland, Sydney, and Western Australia

- C9 in China: Fudan, Shanghai Jiao Tong, Peking, Tsinghua, Harbin, Nanjing, USTC, Xi'an Jiaotong, Zhejiang
- The Russell Group of 24 universities in the UK: Cambridge, Oxford, LSE, UCL, Imperial, etc.
- The "Grande École" business schools in France: about three dozen institutions

The M7 in the US is more relevant than the Ivy League of the eight oldest and most prestigious East Coast private universities, as some of the Ivy Leagues do not even have business schools (Princeton and Brown), while Stanford and the two Chicago schools are "heavy hitters" in the MBA rankings. Other significant exceptions with a strong influence in the MBA space are London Business School (which is not part of the Russell Group) and CEIBS (which is not a member of C9 in China).

Summary

Rankings and accreditations serve somewhat different purposes, which can be summarized with two metaphors:

Rankings are like a bamboo forest: bamboo grows over 10 meters tall, so it is visible from afar; however, it has shallow roots that are no more than a meter deep. This is analogous to the high visibility of rankings, set in contrast with the small number of factors in which they are "rooted."

On the other hand, accreditations are like a vineyard: vines are only 1.5 meters tall, so not particularly visible, but their roots can go 5–10 meters deep. This depth is analogous to the depth of research and conversations on which the accreditation process is based.

The metaphors do not end here: bamboo is used as scaffolding in construction, just as rankings are used to support MBA application decisions; while the concentrated output of vineyards is wine, which is analogous to the accreditation reports that distill all the key information from the school.

Ultimately, both rankings and accreditations are tools that can inform your decision and choice of MBA programs. However, they should not be your only consideration and, as with all tools, they will take time and effort to learn how to utilize them expertly and proficiently.

References

AACSB. (n.d.). *AACSB-accredited schools*. Accessed April 23, 2023, from https://www.aacsb.edu/accredited.

AMBA. (n.d.). *AMBA-accredited business schools*. Accessed July 19, 2023, from https://www.associationofmbas.com/business-schools/accreditation/accredited-schools/.

Byrne, J. (2023, February 12). Financial Times 2023 MBA Ranking: The biggest bombshell is Wharton's disappearance. *Poets & Quants*. Accessed February 12, 2023, from https://poetsandquants.com/2023/02/12/financial-times-2023-mba-ranking/.

EQUIS. (n.d.). *EQUIS accredited schools*. Accessed April 23, 2023, from https://www.efmdglobal.org/accreditations/business-schools/equis/equis-accredited-schools/.

Jack, A., Cremonezi, L. & Stephens, S. (2023, February 12). Global MBA ranking 2023: Methodology update and entry criteria. *The Financial Times*. Accessed February 12, 2023, from https://www.ft.com/mba-method.

Ortmans, L. (2018, January 1). Asian business schools on the rise. *The Financial Times*. Accessed April 19, 2023, from https://www.ft.com/content/c17c448c-d5e6-11e7-a303-9060cb1e5f44.

QS University Rankings. (n.d.) University rankings. Accessed April 19, 2023, from https://www.topuniversities.com/university-rankings.

The Financial Times. (2023). Business school rankings. *The Financial Times*. Accessed April 19, 2023, from https://rankings.ft.com/home/masters-in-business-administration.

The Financial Times. (n.d.) Methodology. *The Financial Times*. Accessed March 3, 2023, from https://rankings.ft.com/methodology.

Top MBA. (2022, September 29). QS global MBA rankings: Methodology. *Top MBA*. Accessed March 3, 2023, from https://www.topmba.com/mba-rankings/methodology.

University of Pennsylvania. (2021). *TTCSP global go to think tank index reports*. Accessed May 14, 2023, from https://repository.upenn.edu/think_tanks/.

4

What a Business School Looks for in an MBA Applicant

MBA Admission Patterns

Have you heard of the proverbial "T-shaped people" whose skillset is shaped like the letter "T": having a breadth of knowledge across various disciplines (the horizontal stroke of "T") and depth of specialization in one particular area (the vertical stroke)? They are the ideal employees of consulting firms: interesting and knowledgeable team players, but at the same time specialist enough so that their skills have value for the organization.

Roughly, this is the type of applicant business schools would ideally like for their MBA programs. However, business schools not only select such people; the MBA programs also help develop T-shaped people. The irony is that you are more likely to emerge as a T-shaped person out of the MBA if you entered the program as a T-shaped person in the first place.

Just as some famous bars and restaurants have their own signature cocktails, so do famous business schools differ in what mix of features they look for in their ideal MBA applicants. Harvard Business School is known for (with or without justification) its "3M"-heavy student profile: McKinsey, Military, Mormons.[1] Typically, full-time MBA programs

---

[1] The Economist (2008).

(especially those delivered in English) have a global market to recruit from, so they have more scope for selecting their ideal candidates and a bigger pool in which to "fish." On the other hand, the market reach of most part-time programs is typically limited to the city or region where they are delivered, as part-time MBA students keep their job while studying. This means applications for part-time MBAs are less competitive and such programs are more often "applicant takers" rather than "applicant shapers." Just look at the acceptance rates at the full-time MBA programs of the top US business schools: Stanford Graduate School of Business is always the most competitive to enter, with only 6.2% of full-time MBA applicants receiving an admission offer in 2021 and 93.6% of those admitted accepting the offer to enroll (the so-called yield rate). For the same year, the Harvard MBA had a 12.5% acceptance rate and an 82.7% yield; while the MIT MBA had a 12.1% acceptance rate but only a 52.4% yield.[2] Harvard admitted one out of every eight applicants (and rejected seven out of eight), while Stanford admitted one out of every 16 applicants (and rejected 15 of the 16). This is in contrast with the application statistics of the less competitive and more regional/local part-time MBA programs, where the majority of applicants are admitted—sometimes even the overwhelming majority.

Eight Key Features

So what are the key factors that business schools consider when making admission decisions for their MBA class? Below is a summary of the eight key dimensions that business schools look for in an MBA applicant. Clearly, you do not need to ace all eight categories to get in: more of one can compensate for less of another. For example, if you score really high on the GMAT test (e.g., over 750 points, which would put you among the top 2% of all test takers), you could get admitted by a top business school even if your career has not been stellar so far—which is a pattern typical of bright young applicants who have not had the time to unleash their career potential. And vice versa: if you are the CEO of a company,

---

[2] Ethier (2022).

your undergraduate academic results and GMAT score become almost irrelevant.

1. Academic Prowess

We warned you in Chap. 1 that MBA detractors will try to convince you that the MBA abbreviation stands for "mediocre but arrogant." However, at least the mediocrity claim can be easily refuted on academic grounds: most leading business schools typically require a solid undergraduate diploma (e.g., GPA of 3.7 out of 4.0 in the US system or a 2:1 degree in the British system) as well as a GMAT score above 600–650 out of 800 points (wherever required, usually for full-time MBAs.) In the 2021 MBA intake, the median GMAT score of those admitted at Stanford was 738 points and the median for Harvard was 730 points.[3] In the same year, the lowest GMAT score with which someone was admitted at Harvard was 590 points (which suggests that person must have really excelled in other areas to compensate for their relatively lackluster GMAT). Achieving a GMAT score of 730 would put you in the 96th percentile, which means being in the top 4% of all who took the test, according to the official GMAT statistics (while the average/mean score of all test takers for 2019–2021 was 575 points).[4]

Academic requirements are partly justified by the academic rigor of the programs and the pressure that the MBA puts on participants: students are expected to enter with a certain level of academic preparedness, essay-writing skills, and a minimum threshold of quantitative and verbal (reasoning) skills. To put it bluntly, if there is even a single person in the classroom who is significantly below the level of the others (the proverbial "squeaky wheel"), they could drag down the level of discussions and waste the time of the professors, potentially jeopardizing the learning process for all students.

At the same time, in addition to signaling intelligence, achieving good grades in a bachelor's program also signals a number of features that are relevant to your future employability, including hard work and discipline, and an ability to fit in a systemic organization and hierarchy. These are

---

[3] Skikne (2022).
[4] MBA.com (n.d.).

traits that employers value and a good undergraduate degree serves as an indicator for having them—in some industries even more so than in others. For example, consultants in particular are expected to be agreeable/easy-going and not at all contrarian; while disagreeableness is more likely to be valued in entrepreneurial circles.

The good news here is that if your GPA/bachelor's diploma is not particularly impressive, you can compensate by putting in more effort in achieving a high GMAT score. Applicants are even encouraged by admission officers to play this game. You can reason in your application essay perfectly plausibly that even though you may not have achieved the greatest diploma, your solid 670 points GMAT score proves that you can cope with the pressures of the MBA perfectly well. Most remarkably, a high GMAT score may serve you even beyond the MBA: strategy consulting firms are known to boast to their clients with the average GMAT score of the consulting team sent on the client's premises. Hopefully, this will give you some encouragement while preparing for the GMAT exam. We recommend investing roughly 200 hours/three months to max out your GMAT score potential.

We can visualize these academic thresholds with a metaphor: imagine the MBA program as a microwave oven. When you put corn in it and turn on the timer, after a few minutes you get popcorn. However, if you put a raw egg in the microwave, the pressure builds up until the egg bursts. The minimum academic threshold for an MBA ensures that the students who enter are the variety of corn ripe for popping, not raw eggs.

2. Career Success

You may have heard the phrase "nothing succeeds like success." MBA programs help you get your next great job but business schools know very well that it is much easier to place in a dream job someone who has already been successful in their career in the first place. You do not need to be the CEO of a company to apply for an MBA but you should be able to show that you have been entrusted with at least some managerial responsibilities in your career so far. We listed in Chap. 1 the four categories of managerial experience that London Business School considers when making an admission offer (managing people, budgets, projects, and processes). With the phenomenal growth of technology companies in the last decade, "product management" has also increased in importance, as it encompasses the whole sequence from product development to product positioning and pricing. With this in mind, you should use your application essays to highlight as much as possible your professional successes rather than tell personal stories that may not enhance your professional credentials.

Your success and seniority in your previous career can also help you decide between a two-year and a one-year full-time MBA. US-style two-year programs can serve better people who aim for a career change (thanks to the longer duration and the internship opportunity between the two years); so by allowing more time to prepare and apply for jobs, these programs can accommodate younger applicants with less-than-stellar past career experience. On the other hand, one-year MBA programs serve better people who aim to accelerate their current career, so admissions officers are more likely to scrutinize more closely and give more weight to their professional successes so far.

3. Job Placeability

Your post-MBA career prospects are clearly related to (and correlated with) your pre-MBA career, even if you may want to change industry or function. Yet some career trajectories easily cross industry and corporate boundaries. For example, engineers and military officers are easy to place in banking and consulting jobs, while artists and philosophers would struggle to get hired for a role that has a quantitative dimension. Similarly, an accountant going for an accounting role would be a shoo-in; and an investment banker can switch into strategy consulting relatively easily—and vice versa.

If you plan to change your career trajectory or change country post-MBA, you should be particularly careful to reassure the admissions officers that you have backup plans in case your ideal scenario does not pan out. For example, you could highlight your willingness to go back to your old industry or to return to your country of origin as Plan B and Plan C.

The MBA career advisers at the school's Career Center often have a say in admission matters and may even be incentivized based on their record of placing MBA students into jobs. This is why an applicant with a solid trajectory of several years of work experience (with managerial responsibilities towards the end) would appear more attractive for admission than a bright fresh graduate.

4. Solvency

MBA fees are high for a reason: the MBA is a premium educational product. For the 2023 intake, the full-time MBA tuition fee at INSEAD is 97,000 euros and the fee at London Business School (LBS) is 109,700 pounds.[5] Moreover, even though there are some scholarships available, most MBA students are expected to pay for their studies in full. The LBS website lists around 100 different scholarship schemes available for its full-time MBA alone (some of these are LBS-only scholarships that come from an allocated pot of LBS funding, while others are national funds/foundations that support students from a given nationality).[6] However, you should consider yourself lucky if you are offered a scholarship/bursary/discount by a top school; while it is actually the mid-tier schools that are typically more willing to offer discounts from the list price under the form of a scholarship.

Schools generally do not care if you will be paying your tuition fees from your own savings, by taking an education loan or if a family member will pay for you. To ensure commitment, schools will usually ask for a deposit of several thousand USD/Euro to be paid soon after receiving the admission letter. The very top schools have loan relationships with local banks, so an admission offer is enough of a guarantee to get you a loan (even for an international student)—but these are only a handful of institutions. All other schools leave your financial arrangements to you. As an example of what options a top school offers, INSEAD lists seven possible loan solutions for admitted MBA students under its Global INSEAD Loans arrangements.[7] One of these is the loans platform Prodigy Finance, which was launched by INSEAD alumni in 2007 as a

---

[5] London Business School (n.d.-a).
[6] London Business School (n.d.-b).
[7] INSEAD Loans (n.d.).

peer-to-peer lending network for fellow-alumni, but has since grown to offer tuition loans for admitted students at 850 educational institutions worldwide.[8]

The MBA admissions process at a mid-tier school can be an interesting example of "price elasticity" in action: your application to the school is typically an "open kimono" where you disclose your career progression in detail (hence your income bracket will be known), so the admissions officers can gauge your willingness to pay. If they want you in their MBA class, they can adjust the MBA fee down by throwing in a scholarship/discount as a sweetener to bring you over the line. So make sure to signal that you are strongly interested in the scholarship options to open the negotiation channel with the school.

If you plan to apply for scholarships, you should submit your MBA application early in the cycle. In the later stages, schools typically take off their waitlist only people who can pay the full fee. It would not be a good time to start a negotiation if you are admitted in the last round.

5. Company Sponsorship

There are good reasons why business schools like company-sponsored students. If you come in with company sponsorship, you already have two endorsements in your quiver: (i) pre-selection: Your employer deems you worthy of the cost (and hassle) of sending you to do an MBA; and (ii) pre-authorization: The financial package removes the need to negotiate down your tuition fees. (Companies generally do not haggle as hard as individuals do when it comes to a payment of USD 100,000.)

Schools also like company-sponsored students as they create a relationship between the school and the company that can lead to job placements for other graduates and research opportunities for professors (who may gain access to the company's data trove to write a journal paper or to produce a case study). A single company-sponsored student may evolve into a multi-year arrangement for multiple employees, for both MBA and other degree programs as well as for executive education (which is often the highest-margin product delivered by a business school).

---

[8] Prodigy Finance (n.d.).

Typically, company sponsorship is more relevant for part-time MBAs. Full-time MBAs rarely get company sponsorship unless they are working for a leading strategy consultancy/investment bank/global conglomerate, or for the US army—all of which have established sponsorship practices. Family-owned firms also sponsor the studies of the next generation of the family because it is simply tax-efficient to pay from the pre-tax revenue rather than from the post-tax income.

Even if your employer is not willing to pay for your studies, ask them if a "salary sacrifice scheme" would be possible in your jurisdiction (it would depend on the tax rules in the country). Under such a scheme, the company retains a portion of your gross salary and pays your tuition fees from it as a company expense—so the fee is paid from your pre-tax salary, rather than from your post-tax net income.

EMBA students are typically the ones who are more often company-sponsored (as are many participants in Executive Education). If you join an EMBA program where the majority of participants are paying their program fees themselves, you may have joined a part-time MBA that is being (mis)branded as an EMBA for marketing purposes.

6. Diversity

Gender, nationality, ethnicity, and LGBT+ status are key dimensions that most leading business schools will try to take into account. Gender balance in an MBA class is the dream of many program directors. Therefore, if you are a woman or belong to an under-represented nationality or minority, you may have better chances of admission at most business schools. The only major exception to this rule is China where women do not get privileged access anymore as Chinese MBA programs already have more than 50% female students in the classroom.[9]

Some organizations have their primary focus on diversity and can help you identify the more "enlightened" schools or opportunities. Examples are The Athena SWAN accreditation framework (originally an abbreviation for Scientific Women's Academic Network), which now works

---

[9] Allen (2020).

towards gender equality in higher education in general,[10] as well as the Forte Foundation, which gives MBA scholarships to women once they are accepted at one of the 55 participating top US and European business schools.[11]

Business schools often have their own incentives and formal or informal quotas aimed at promoting diversity. So even if the school where you are applying does not have an explicit list of merit-based/diversity scholarships, you should ask them what they do for diversity. Even if this does not help your admission prospects, at least you can be assured that you will be studying in a diverse class.

7. Exceptional Achievements and Leadership

You do not need to be an Olympic medal winner to apply for a top MBA program—but it helps. Some of the very top full-time MBA programs turn down nine out of 10 applicants, so being exceptional makes you stand out by definition. Exceptionality/distinctiveness comes in many shapes and sizes, for example sports champions, decorated veterans, successful entrepreneurs, prize-winning charity leaders, media celebrities (including social influencers). However, do not worry too much if you do not fall into the outlier category: some 98% of successful MBA applicants are most likely not world-leading in any way. Yet, it is important to highlight every piece of leadership and achievement in your CV/resume: every marathon completed, mountain peak hiked, work team led, community project organized, etc. The best thing about it is that you can train for a marathon and complete it in less than a year; or think of and launch an initiative that you can lead in an even shorter time frame. So, as you are ramping up your MBA application plans, you can start creating distinctive (and genuine) content for your CV for all the good reasons.

Nyenrode Business University in the Netherlands has three core values, which can be useful to any MBA applicant: Leadership, Entrepreneurship, Stewardship.[12] So go through your CV and highlight

---

[10] Athena Swan Charter (n.d.).
[11] Forte Foundation (n.d.).
[12] Nyenrode Business Universiteit (n.d.).

when you 1) led teams; 2) started new things; 3) mentored others. These can also serve as a foundation for some of your application essays.

8. Entrepreneurial Zeal

Entrepreneurship has been a particularly hot topic at business schools in the last decade so it deserves a special mention here. You do not even need to have succeeded as an entrepreneur: entrepreneurial failure counts as well (provided you spin it as a learning journey, rather than moan about the unfairness of the world). You do not even need to have founded a start-up to prove you have an entrepreneurial spirit: starting new things counts, whether these are new projects in your job, new initiatives in your neighborhood, or taking the lead in organizing your high school's alumni reunion. While preparing for a marathon may take you up to a year, registering your own company takes less than an hour in most Western countries and has a negligible cost (GBP 12 when done online in the UK).[13] So if you have any ideas for a start-up, you could consider launching that start-up before you apply for the MBA and then talk about it in your essays. The best thing about founding a company is that it is a win–win strategy: the start-up may either lead to something new (though not necessarily big—bear in mind that most start-ups fail anyway),[14] or you get valuable experience that can become one of your application essay stories. However, there is a caveat: check with your current employer or in your employment contract that you are allowed to serve as a company director (which would be your role by definition as the owner of a company).

Entrepreneurship is also related to curiosity and creativity, so if you never did anything entrepreneurial, you could at least highlight in your application essays stories from your life and career that portray you as a dynamic and interesting person. Therefore, it is never too late to start writing a blog on a topic of interest to you or set up a curated Instagram page on a theme.

---

[13] Government UK (n.d.).
[14] Eisenmann (2021).

Summary

We can summarize the eight categories of features that business schools look for into three broad groups: 1) Intelligence and academic achievement; 2) Career success and financial stability; and 3) Distinctiveness. We should also reinforce our earlier message that all these categories are relative and you do not need to be a star in every dimension. Admission into a leading MBA is a holistic process and everything counts: if you get more "points" on the swings, you would not need as many "points" on the roundabouts. If you are reading this book, it is quite likely that by virtue of its topic and your own self-selection process (interest in an MBA), you are already a "T-shaped person." Therefore, it is important that you bring all your key qualities to the fore and present vividly and convincingly how your "T" has been formed by your education and developed in your professional career. We discuss in the next chapter how to "dot the i's and cross the t's" of the MBA application process.

References

Allen, N. (2020, December 9). The most gender equitable MBA programs are in ... China?. *Poets & Quants*. Accessed April 14, 2023, from https://poetsandquants.com/2020/12/09/the-most-gender-equitable-mba-programs-are-in-china/.

Athena Swan Charter. (n.d.). *Homepage*. Accessed April 14, 2023, from https://www.advance-he.ac.uk/equality-charters/athena-swan-charter.

Eisenmann, T. (2021). Why start-ups fail. *Harvard Business Review*. Accessed April 15, 2023, from https://hbr.org/2021/05/why-start-ups-fail.

Ethier, M. (2022, April 22). 'The Window' closes: Acceptance rates at the top 50 U.S. MBA programs. *Poets & Quants*. Accessed April 14, 2023, from https://poetsandquants.com/2022/04/02/the-window-closes-acceptance-rates-at-the-top-50-u-s-mba-programs/.

Forte Foundation. (n.d.). *Homepage*. Accessed April 14, 2023, from https://www.fortefoundation.org/site/SPageServer/?pagename=partners_bschool.

Government UK. (n.d.) *Register your company*. Accessed April 15, 2023, from https://www.gov.uk/limited-company-formation/register-your-company.

INSEAD. (n.d.) *Global INSEAD loans.* Accessed April 15, 2023, from https://www.insead.edu/master-programmes/mba/financing/external-funding.

London Business School. (n.d.-a). *Fees, financing and scholarships.* Accessed April 15, 2023, from https://www.london.edu/masters-degrees/mba/fees-financing-and-scholarships.

London Business School. (n.d.-b). *Search for funding.* Accessed April 15, 2023, from https://www.london.edu/masters-degrees/financial-aid/search-for-funding.

MBA.com. (n.d.) GMAT: Understanding your score. *MBA.* Accessed April 15, 2023, from https://www.mba.com/exams/gmat-exam/scores/understanding-your-score.

Nyenrode Business Universiteit. (n.d.) *Core values.* Accessed April 15, 2023, from https://www.nyenrode.nl/en/about-nyenrode/core-values.

Prodigy Finance. (n.d.) *Homepage.* Accessed April 15, 2023, from https://prodigyfinance.com.

Skikne, C. (2022, February 8). What GMAT score do you need for Harvard?. *BusinessBecause.* Accessed April 15, 2023, from https://www.businessbecause.com/news/gmat/6930/gmat-score-for-harvard.

The Economist. (2008, August 7). Factory for unhappy people. *The Economist.* Accessed May 8, 2023 from https://www.economist.com/books-and-arts/2008/08/07/factory-for-unhappy-people.

5

How Do You Apply for Your Ideal MBA Program

Eight Steps to Lift-Off

Think of your MBA application process as the launch of a rocket into space. The first day of class is the moment of lift-off. However, what precedes this moment is years of research and development (R&D). Below is our eight-step guide to preparing for and breezing through the MBA application process to reach the moment of successful lift-off: accepting an admission offer from your top-choice business school and starting the MBA program. You may need to spend 2 years on this process, split 50–50 between the "R" and the "D" of R&D: a year to research your ideal schools and programs and a year to develop your application to bring it to its optimal state.

1. Gather Information About the MBA
We discussed in Chap. 1 the eight key motivations for doing an MBA. Hopefully, these can help you decide if the MBA is the right program for you, compared with alternatives such as a postgraduate degree in law, data science, digital marketing, etc.; professional qualifications

such as CFA, CIMA, ACCA, CIM; or simply no postgraduate degree/qualification at all.

As part of the information-gathering process, you should read all relevant articles on Wikipedia (including the "Criticism"/"Controversies" section at the bottom—bearing in mind that MBA programs hold critical thinking in high regard); subscribe to MBA-related content, e.g., on Apple News, Google Alerts, Poets & Quants, BusinessBecause, etc.; join social media groups (GMAT Club, LinkedIn MBA alumni groups—if they will let you in); and talk to MBA graduates. In researching the MBA delivery mode that is right for you, you can refer to the list of formats we presented in Chap. 2 (full-time, part-time, online, blended).

A word of warning on Mini-MBAs: just as a vodka martini is five parts vodka and one part martini, a mini-MBA is five parts "mini" and one part MBA. Most mini-MBAs offer a random smattering of business knowledge that, even if useful, cannot be compared to the breadth and depth of content, interaction, and experiences that a proper MBA provides. Having said that, there are some good "stackable certificate-type" offerings on the market. The "MBA Essentials" of the London School of Economics is a 10-subjects-in-10-weeks program for GBP 3200—a great taster menu if you are uncertain about pursuing a proper MBA and would like to learn more before you commit.[1]

2. Identify the Key Criteria to Optimize your Choice

When you start researching your options for where to do an MBA, you should consider the range of factors that we introduced in Chap. 2. The key ones are location (countries and cities); types of schools (private or public); fees (as a proxy for quality); institutional networks; alumni networks and career trajectories; and areas of distinctiveness and reputation for specialization. Given their importance, we dedicated rankings and accreditations to a separate chapter (Chap. 3). Below we expand and recap on two crucial dimensions: location and fees.

Our key advice on location is: try to do your MBA in the country or the city where you would like to be based after graduation. Even business

---

[1] LSE (n.d.).

schools with a global reputation (Harvard, Stanford, LBS, INSEAD) have their strongest network of alumni and corporate contacts around their home campus. Having said that, you should also do your research on the work visa formalities for working in the country if you do not have the respective country's citizenship. Most Western countries give a "no-questions-asked" work permit for a year or two after completing an MBA from a reputable institution in that country, but this would still leave you dependent on your future employer for work visa sponsorship for a number of years beyond that.

Since the UK left the European Union in 2020, we have noticed a dip in the number of EU students going to Britain as their work options in the UK have been curtailed post-Brexit.[2] On the other hand, with the growth of the Asian economies and the rise of Asian business schools, there is increasing interest in the MBAs in Asia's global cities such as Singapore, Hong Kong, and Shanghai. The 2023 Financial Times Global MBA ranking (of full-time MBAs) included 19 Asia-Pacific schools: 6 in India, 5 in Singapore, 3 in Mainland China, 3 in Hong Kong, 1 in South Korea, and 1 in Australia;[3] compared with 13 Asian schools in the 2012 ranking.[4] In the EMBA space, the rise of Asia has been even more pronounced: 32 of the Top-100 EMBA programs in the 2022 Financial Times EMBA ranking were delivered partly or fully in Asia (including Australia and the Middle East);[5] compared with 25 in the 2012 ranking.[6]

The second aspect that is of key importance to most MBA applicants are the fees. In the MBA world, tuition fees are seen as a proxy for quality: the higher the fee, the better the institution and the program are perceived to be. Unfortunately, there is no "free lunch" here: the majority of MBA students pay the asking price (or close to the asking price, give or take a bursary/discount that may be offered by the school). In the UK, MBA fees at accredited programs start from around USD25,000[7] (especially those subsidized under a UK Government-funded apprenticeship

---

[2] O'Carroll and Adams (2023).
[3] The Financial Times (2023).
[4] The Financial Times (2012a).
[5] The Financial Times (2022).
[6] The Financial Times (2012b).
[7] De Novellis (2021).

scheme) and go up to around USD200,000 for the EMBA programs of LBS and LSE.[8]

When you have carefully considered all the aspects we suggested and are ready to apply, whittle down your shortlist of target business schools to five:

- One dream school (your stretch goal)
- Three ambitious but realistic schools (ones likely to admit you)
- One safe school (where you are sure to get in)

3. Time Your MBA Application

When is a good time to apply for an MBA? The typical ages at which people apply for the different formats of the MBA are:

- 25–30 for a Full-time MBA
- 27–35 for a Part-time MBA (Evening/Weekend format)
- 30–45 for an Executive MBA (typically in Modular format)
- 25–45 for an Online MBA

Obviously, if you are not within these ideal age ranges, you may have a thousand other valid reasons to apply for an MBA. We have seen 70-year-old MBA students in Japan and Latin America who did very well.

We recommend at least 3 years of work experience (the minimum requirement for an AMBA-accredited MBA) by the time your MBA is planned to start. This ensures maturity but also sufficient experience so that you are able to discuss matters of practice in the classroom, rather than learn everything as theory. Institutions with long admission cycles (e.g., LBS, INSEAD, and the leading US schools) typically require 2 years upon application (e.g., in September), with the assumption that you will continue working for up to a year until the program starts (e.g., in September the following year). Some US schools admit a number of top graduates of their own undergraduate business program straight into the MBA without requiring them to go out and gain work experience,

---

[8] Nugent (2021).

primarily because they do not want to lose them to other MBA programs if they have to wait for 3 years.

At the leading strategy consulting firms (McKinsey, BCG, Bain), there is an implicit expectation that young consultants will go away for a full-time MBA after 2 years in the job and their MBAs are usually company-sponsored. Many investment bankers also do an MBA after their first couple of years at the bank, but the prevalence is not as high as in strategy consulting. People working in investment banking tend to disclose to their boss that they are applying for business school only after they have received their annual bonus (for obvious reasons).

A paradox of the MBA is that its different formats can be both cyclical and counter-cyclical. When a recession hits and many young professionals lose their job, full-time MBA programs suddenly start to receive a lot more applicants. On the other hand, when the economy is growing, working executives tend to stay in their jobs, so part-time MBA and EMBA programs get a boost. Yet, you should not be intimidated by the economic cycle as application numbers and the degree of competitiveness change only by a few percentage points year-on-year. So time your application with your own life and career cycle.

Schools that have clear MBA admission cycles with strict deadlines are typically the most competitive and prestigious ones. At the other end of the spectrum, there are schools/programs with permanent rolling admission, which suggests they are open to anyone to join if they can pay their tuition fees. In the latter case, you may want to recall the Groucho Marx maxim: "I don't want to belong to any club that would have me as a member." Your admission into an MBA should ideally come as the fulfillment of a stretch goal after a sustained and momentous effort, rather than as easily as "a walk in the park."

4. Plan Your References

MBA programs usually ask for two references and these should both be professional (based on your work). When you are considering who can give you the best endorsement, you should balance seniority at the organization against proximity to you. People often pick the CEO, but if the CEO cannot say much about you (whether positive or negative), this will be seen by the admissions officer as poor social skills and a lack of self-awareness on your part.

If you would like to "groom" a high-ranking executive for a reference but are not particularly close to them, you could ask them a year earlier to become your mentor. In this way, you will establish a much closer connection and will gain valuable insights, while also giving them visibility of who you are.

A frequently asked question is: How much can you guide the referee on what to write in the reference letter? You can remind them of your key points and achievements, but do not force them or expect them to sign off on the text that you have prepared. This can backfire in multiple ways: from sounding like a self-produced reference; to your referee disclosing your attempts to doctor the process to the business school.

5. Take the GMAT/GRE

The leading full-time MBA programs in the world require one of the standardized admission tests: GMAT or GRE. GMAT was traditionally designed with MBA programs in mind, while the GRE was originally meant for graduate study in a range of disciplines. However, the two seem to overlap more and more at business schools and most institutions now accept both. The GMAT exam has four sections (Quantitative Reasoning, Verbal Reasoning, Integrated Reasoning, and Analytical Writing Assessment); takes 3 h and 7 min; and costs USD275 if taken at a test center or USD250 if taken online.[9] The GRE has three sections (Quantitative Reasoning, Verbal Reasoning, Analytical Writing); takes 3 h and 45 min; and costs USD205 (at a test center or online).[10]

The organization that runs the GMAT has been offering a lighter version of the test called Executive Assessment (EA)[11] since 2016, which is used primarily for admission into EMBA programs. EA has three sections: Integrated Reasoning, Verbal Reasoning, and Quantitative Reasoning; it takes only 90 min in total; and costs USD350 (at a test

---

[9] MBA.com (n.d.-b).
[10] ETS.org (n.d.).
[11] MBA.com (n.d.-a).

center or online). Another shorter version of the GMAT, called GMAT Focus Edition, will be launched in late 2023 and will be offered in parallel with the existing GMAT version. GMAT Focus Edition will take 135 min in total, evenly divided into three sections: Quantitative Reasoning, Verbal Reasoning, and Data Insights.[12]

If your program does not require a standardized test score, this would make your application process easier. However, having the barriers to entry so much lower would also make things easier for everybody else. An MBA with low admission standards is by definition a lower-quality experience. So, do your best to get into the most demanding "club" that would let you in.

Typically, EMBAs for senior executives do not require any standardized test. However, rest assured, programs for senior executives would not be of lower quality as there are two substantive thresholds in place already: a senior role requirement and the high EMBA tuition fee (a proxy for career success).

We discussed in Chap. 4 the various GMAT cut-off points and percentiles. You should plan to spend at least 3 months preparing for the GMAT to reach your full potential, practicing tests online or on paper daily (1–2 h a day would be ideal if you can allocate this amount of time). It helps to identify early on your strengths and weaknesses; it will largely depend on your high school or college background if you find the math or the verbal section more challenging.

While this is not sound advice in life, it is the best advice for acing the GMAT: focus on your weaknesses. You need to keep doing over and over again the types of problems/questions you get wrong until you can answer correctly every question at your stretch-goal difficulty level (remember, the test is adaptive: the more hard questions you answer, the more questions at that level and higher you will receive). This will help you get accustomed to a higher level of difficulty that will push up the ceiling in the adaptive algorithm of the test during the real exam.

When you create an account on the MBA.com website (the official site of the GMAT test), you are given access to various preparatory materials as well as the option to take two official GMAT Test Exams for free. You

---

[12] MBA.com (n.d.-c).

can pay USD108 to take up to four more official GMAT tests. Since the Covid-19 pandemic, the official GMAT test can also be taken online (or at 1 of 650 testing centers around the world, as before). There is also a free downloadable smartphone app GMAT Official Practice, which can be handy in doing practice questions on the move.

If you score reasonably well in the GMAT (650 out of the 800 maximum points would put you in the top 30% of test takers),[13] you would be an attractive applicant for most business schools. A score above 700 points (putting you in the top 13%) would give you a strong reason to bargain for (i.e., request politely) a scholarship/tuition fee discount. Since you are allowed to send your GMAT score for free to up to five schools, hedge your bets between dream schools, realistic schools, and safe schools.

Separately from the GMAT/GRE, many MBA programs taught in English also require language tests for non-native speakers. The main exams are TOEFL (US) and IELTS (UK). However, if you have a prior degree completed in English, business schools will accept this as proof of language fluency and waive the English language test requirement. The language test itself is not a major differentiating factor but merely a hygiene threshold—you simply need to pass the minimum requirement, e.g., 90–100 points (out of 120) in TOEFL or 6.5–7.0 points (out of 9.0) in IELTS.

6. Polish Your CV/Resume

Your Curriculum Vitae (CV), also known as your Resume in the USA, is your life story at a glance. It should never be more than two pages long (US business schools even prefer a single page, especially for younger applicants). Try to be strategic in what you include in your CV and present your career and life history through the lens of a self-directed autonomous and impactful executive rather than someone who merely took orders. Junior people often talk about tasks and responsibilities in their CVs, while senior people talk about measuring their impact with metrics (e.g., investments achieved, sales generated), designing strategies, and managing teams. There is no harm in trying to quantify everything you

---

[13] MBA.com (n.d.-d).

have achieved but be realistic: a 24-year-old in a sales role is not expected to be generating the entire company's revenue of hundreds of millions of dollars.

In terms of formatting, the Europass CV template may not be an ideal option as it wastes space and can result in a 3–4 page long CV. Go for a US-style resume template that is highly skimmable, e.g., one that lists your company and position on the left in two lines; and years of work and location (City, Country) symmetrically on the right (for example, the downloadable template recommended by Harvard).[14] The content of your job should be listed in 3–5 bullet points underneath. This format gives the best "at a glance" experience to the interviewer, as it creates a timeline (with dates and locations) on the right-hand side of the page. Once it is in the right format, ask a friend (ideally an HR professional) to have a look and give you some objective feedback. Remember to always list some personal interests at the bottom to add color to your CV and make yourself more memorable. You can merge all content from "Leadership & Activities" into a broader "Additional Information, Skills & Interests" section at the very end. In that part, make sure that what you write is not generic and bland (e.g., "I like reading and running"), but rather factual, detailed, and demonstrates your drive (e.g., "organizer of the Galaxy science fiction reading club"; "completed Boston marathon in 2023"; "ran 150 times with ParkRun London in 2021–2023").

7. Write the Application Essays

Five is the number of schools that can be nominated for free to receive your GMAT score but also a reasonable set of application essays that you can manage in an application round.

Typically, a business school will ask for 2–3 application essays. The questions or parts of the questions will often repeat: "Why an MBA? Why here? Where do you want to be in 5 years? Was there a time when you led others? How do you measure your impact? Have you overcome any obstacles or adversity? How much do you value diversity?"

---

[14] Harvard (n.d.).

You should be able to re-purpose parts of the essays for multiple applications, but make sure to run a keyword search to stop you from inadvertently telling Harvard that you are thrilled to be applying at Stanford.

Admissions officers appreciate a clear and straightforward story, so cut out unnecessary details and simplify your storyline, just as flower shops trim the leaves of a flower before they sell it to you. If you want to be a strategy consultant after your MBA, tell a clear linear story about what you have already achieved along the strategy consulting trajectory and where you want the MBA to take you. Communications professionals recommend the STAR storytelling format (situation, task, action, result)[15] for anything you have done in the past: try to mock up the backbone of the story in four sentences that you can then elaborate on where necessary. However, a modification we recommend for an MBA application is SOAR (situation, obstacle, action, result). Our SOAR format will nudge you towards choosing stories that highlight your achievements despite all the difficulties that life throws in.

Ideally, all your essays should describe professional situations or demonstrate relevance to your career. You want to highlight that you are a driven professional—not an entertainer with a set of fun stories. And, just as with your CV, give your essays to a friend to read through and take their feedback on board.

8. Ace the Interview

In the past, MBA admission interviews used to be held face-to-face by an admissions officer touring the world or a local alum of the MBA program; and applicants were expected to travel to the main campus or to a major city for the interview. Since the Covid-19 pandemic, however, many of the interviews are conducted online. Yet, if you are visiting the business school for an open day, nothing can beat the experience of an in-person interview.

In all top MBAs, every participant who ultimately is admitted will have been interviewed (but this does not mean that everyone who applies

---

[15] Carnegie Mellon University (n.d.).

will get an interview). If you receive an interview invitation, this is definitely a good sign that you are on track to being admitted.

There is no definitive answer to the question: Should you discuss with an admissions officer where else you are applying? You may be able to skillfully convince them that you are a highly sought-after candidate; but you may also inadvertently signal that you are not fully committed to the institution where you are applying. If in doubt, do not bring up this topic unless they ask you. Playing schools one against the other to elicit better terms in the form of a scholarship or a discount only becomes an option once you have at least two admission offers in your hand.

Just as in any interview, you should be polite and respectful to the interviewer and try to find commonalities between your background and theirs. If you are already a mid-ranking corporate executive, you are likely to be more successful (and powerful) in your career than the admissions officer, so it is important to be kind to them as well. You may be earning more money but they still call the shots about the outcome of your application, so a bit of humility goes a long way.

The interview is also an opportunity for you to ask insightful questions that not only show the depth of your research of the institution but can also be useful to you in making the final decision (if you have multiple offers). Teasing out the distinctiveness of the business school would be a key area to explore with an insider. You could even sprinkle your conversation with creative questions that may not have ever come up before, for example: (1) Can I be given access to the School's AMBA/AACSB/EQUIS accreditation report? (The answer will be "No," but worth trying.) (2) What is the most popular or impactful piece of research ever published by any of the school's faculty? (3) Is there a famous Business Ethics or Sustainability case covered in the curriculum? (4) Do the MBA courses teach more success cases than failure cases?

If the interviewer cannot answer your question, you have succeeded in leaving a positive impression. They will probably commit to finding the answer and emailing it to you, which creates a second point of contact and slightly improves your chances. Either way, do not forget to send your interviewer a "thank you" email the day after the interview, bringing up the one or two most memorable things that you discussed.

Summary

The algorithm of eight steps will fill up much of your spare time during the MBA application process. And if you do not get in at the first attempt, you can always apply the following year and use the months in between to improve your GMAT score, get a promotion at work, take an online course that fills a gap in your academic background, and talk to more alumni. Alumni often feedback their observations on potential candidates to the admissions team, so use this as a back-door tool to get your name mentioned more often. If you do not succeed even on your second attempt, perhaps you should consider changing your target schools. Crucially, you should never get fixated on one single institution: use a basket of five schools of different standing to hedge your bets and improve your prospects of being admitted.

References

Carnegie Mellon University. (n.d.). *How to tell a STAR story?* Accessed April 17, 2023, from https://www.cmu.edu/tepper/alumni/assets/docs/star-story.pdf.

De Novellis, M. (2021, March 11). Top 10 most affordable MBA programs in the UK. *BusinessBecause*. Accessed April 17, 2023, from https://www.businessbecause.com/news/mba-rankings/4760/top-10-most-affordable-mba-programs-uk.

ETS.org. (n.d.). GRE. Accessed April 19, 2023, from https://www.ets.org/gre.html.

Harvard. (n.d.). *Harvard College bullet point resume template*. Accessed April 16, 2023, from https://careerservices.fas.harvard.edu/resources/bullet-point-resume-template/.

LSE. (n.d.). *MBA essentials*. Accessed April 15, 2023, from https://www.lse.ac.uk/study-at-lse/online-learning/courses/mba-essentials.

MBA.com. (n.d.-a). Executive assessment. *MBA*. Accessed April 19, 2023, from https://www.mba.com/exams/executive-assessment.

MBA.com. (n.d.-b). GMAT. *MBA*. Accessed April 19, 2023, from https://www.mba.com/exams/gmat-exam.

MBA.com. (n.d.-c). GMAT focus edition. *MBA*. Accessed April 19, 2023, from https://www.mba.com/exams/gmat-focus-edition/.

MBA.com. (n.d.-d). GMAT: Understanding your score. *MBA*. Accessed April 15, 2023, from https://www.mba.com/exams/gmat-exam/scores/understanding-your-score.

Nugent, T. (2021, July 20). MIT sloan is world's most expensive MBA program in 2021. *BusinessBecause*. Accessed April 17, 2023 from https://www.businessbecause.com/news/mba-cost/6994/mit-sloan-most-expensive-mba-program.

O'Carroll, L., & Adams, R. (2023, January 27). Number of EU students enrolling in UK universities halves post-Brexit. *The Guardian*. Accessed April 15, 2023, from https://www.theguardian.com/education/2023/jan/27/number-eu-students-enrolling-uk-universities-down-half-since-brexit.

The Financial Times. (2012a, January 30). Global MBA rankings 2012. *The Financial Times*. Accessed April 19, 2023, from https://rankings.ft.com/rankings/1071/global-mba-rankings-2012.

The Financial Times. (2012b, October 14). EMBA ranking 2012. *The Financial Times*. Accessed April 15, 2023, from https://rankings.ft.com/rankings/1291/emba-ranking-2012

The Financial Times. (2022, October 16). EMBA 2022 Business School rankings. *The Financial Times*. Accessed April 19, 2023, from https://rankings.ft.com/rankings/2876/emba-2022.

The Financial Times. (2023, February 12). MBA 2023 Business School rankings. *The Financial Times*. Accessed April 19, 2023, from https://rankings.ft.com/rankings/2909/mba-2023.

Part II

Making the Most of Your MBA Studies

6

How to Extract Most Academic Value from Your Business School and MBA Program

The MBA as a Jet Engine

At a conceptual level, the MBA is like a jet engine that uses fuel and oxygen to propel you forward. All things academic are the fuel (courses, projects, cases). All things non-academic and extracurricular are the oxygen (networking, career support, job interviews). And just as in a jet engine, the two need to be mixed in an orderly fashion and ignited for thrust to be generated.

At a more practical level, when you start your MBA you will find that there is an academic director of the program (the captain of the flight) and an operational director/manager (the flight engineer). The balance of power and responsibilities between the two may differ at different institutions but what is important for you is to distinguish between their roles. Therefore, academic problems related to the design of the MBA, course content, exam policy, etc., should be addressed to the academic director; while non-academic issues should be dealt with at the operational level.

Introduction to Eight Academic Areas

In the academic space, we have identified eight (lucky number!) important themes that you need to understand to make the most of your time at business school.

1. Appreciating the Balance between Theory and Practice

As Yogi Berra said: "In theory there is no difference between theory and practice. In practice there is." Practice is key, but you would not be attending an academic institution if theory did not matter. The best academics do not merely lecture theories or plod through case studies; they use theory as a fulcrum to leverage your learning and lead you to an epiphany. At the other end of the scale, the best practitioners do not merely tell "war stories" (as corporate stories are jokingly referred to); they also use theoretical frameworks to make sense of the complexity of the real world.

On the spectrum of "Thinking, Fast and Slow" (Daniel Kahneman's famous book), practitioners are the fast thinkers (they immediately apply things in practice), while researchers are the slow thinkers (they come up with frameworks and try to explain the world). The Association of MBAs (AMBA) requires at least 50% of the MBA-teaching faculty at an institution to be academically qualified doctoral-level graduates (lecturers, associate and full professors). Yet, this leaves up to 50% for practitioners, who often do not have a fancy title—though at some institutions the status of the teaching practitioners may be formalized with a "Professor of Practice" title.

Most leading business schools use "action learning": they give MBA students real practice problems to solve. These are in-company projects nested in a Management Practice or Consultancy course in which groups of MBAs work as a team. Even though many practitioners are involved in these projects in supporting roles (e.g., the executives at the company where the MBA team is doing the consultancy gig), it takes an academic to bring together into a coherent whole the different strands and dimensions of the problem, just as the conductor of an orchestra brings into harmony the various musical instruments and their players.

To give you another metaphorical framework, if theory is the ground, practice is the sky. You might remember from your high school biology class that flight has evolved independently four times in the animal kingdom (in dinosaurs, insects, bats, and birds). Analogously, there are four types of practitioners that business schools bring on campus:

- Company CEOs who give talks as part of "distinguished speaker series" (these are the dinosaurs of the animal world: they are the biggest things that have ever walked on land).
- Guest speakers within a course (these are the butterflies). Some schools such as Zhejiang University School of Management in Hangzhou, China, require each course to include at least four guest speakers (who may get involved in just a part of a lesson/class).
- Consultancy project tutors (these are the bats, moonlighting at night, while keeping a day job in the business world).
- Professors of practice (these are the birds: the full-time fliers "chained to the sky," as Bob Dylan might say).

2. Mastering the Case Method

Business schools are famous for using case studies focused on real companies as their primary teaching tool. Actually, the case method was first applied at Harvard Law School in the late 1800s[1] but business schools adopted it on a large scale to bridge the divide between the academic and the business world.

Some leading schools host vast libraries of case studies developed by their own faculty: Harvard Business School (USA), Ivey Business School (Canada), Cranfield School of Management (UK); Dalian University of Technology's School of Economics and Management (for cases in Chinese/about Chinese companies); and Nagoya University of Commerce and Business (for cases in Japanese).

The case method exists in order to develop a growth mindset: students enhance their abilities by overcoming challenges and discovering solutions, which shapes their learning journey based on their own experience of tackling the case. (On the other hand, giving students the ready answers

---

[1] Banks (2017).

reinforces a fixed mindset, i.e., no growth.) However, in recent years, even case discussions with their Socratic style of debating have been accused of distilling the complexity of the world into a manual, a "guided tour" through the business jungle where students are spoon-fed all the necessary information.

Supporters of the case method focus on the following advantages:

- Cases deal with real companies and everything that happens in a case comes from the business world or the real world.
- Key theoretical points and frameworks are woven into the fabric of the case, so students walk away with conceptual knowledge, not just a "war story" and a vivid example.
- Case discussions force the student to make decisions and defend them to the class, reinforcing communication and leadership skills.
- The classroom debates are lively interactive discussions that can even be entertaining, which wins students' attention and helps them focus.
- The energy in the classroom is palpable, according to all who have been involved or observed a case discussion. Both students and professors get recharged by this energy.

However, opponents bring out some counter-arguments:

- Harvard Business Publishing is the biggest publisher of business case studies in the world, and the companies and cases are largely US-centric.
- The 15–20 page "cooked" cases give you all the necessary information: you are not even supposed/allowed to research the company online to avoid finding out the answers to the case.
- There is a range of fixed solutions in a "cooked" case and these are outlined in the teaching notes, which the professor has at hand (these teaching notes are sometimes longer than the case itself). In this sense, a case discussion is like landing at an international airport: no matter how long and winding the corridors are, you will reach passport control and the baggage reclaim area, just as the case nudges you towards predetermined answers. Columbia Business School in partic-

ular is known as a vocal opponent of the Harvard-style "cooked" case studies.[2]
- Case studies are not a suitable format for developing core technical skills, such as data analysis.
- Some old cases that are considered classics (e.g., from the 1960s) are still widely taught at modern business schools, but in the age of Netflix and Apple, they look stale (what we call "zombie cases").

Some schools encourage their faculty to use the case method in class by introducing minimum case content requirements. In emerging markets (e.g., China) this takes the form of a 2×2 case matrix, where courses may be required to have at least one of each of these four types of cases:

- Local company doing business in the country
- Local company doing business abroad
- Foreign company doing business in the country
- Foreign company doing business abroad

Incidentally, military schools divide the type of cases they teach along another dimension: success vs failure; and they choose to teach a lot more failure cases than success cases. This is based on the rationale that it is easier to learn the right lessons from failure because the number of factors that contribute to failure is limited. Whereas business schools teach a lot more success cases but, counterproductively, it is harder to learn from success as the factors leading to success are much more numerous.

There are three alternatives to the "cooked" case studies that have seen their rate of adoption grow in recent years:

- "Raw" cases: where the students are given 100–200 pages of various documents about the company and have to make up their mind what is important to consider and what to throw away. In a raw case, even the use of shortcuts to deciding which documents to read, given limited time, helps you develop valuable skills.

---

[2] Gloeckler (2008).

- Live cases: where students work on a real company in real-time, discussing with company executives the real problems of the organization, sometimes even while visiting the company's premises. Live cases teach you how to deal with complexity under a range of scenarios, not just in one particular situation. (This has an analogy in the Chinese proverb 授人以鱼不如授人以渔: "Give a man a fish and you feed him for a day; teach a man to fish and you feed him for a lifetime.")
- Mini cases in which a company's challenges are presented in one or two pages, often in the form of a published business newspaper article. Mini cases are used in EMBA programs in particular, as the executive summary format suits busy executives. A mini case can be compared to a pocket map or a map on your smartphone screen: it is easy to access and gives you all the information at a glance. (While a full case study is like rolling out a 3-m long foldable paper map: clearly with a lot more detail in it but with reduced usability.)

One last piece of advice related to the novelty of the cases used in class: If you find that the cases being taught in your MBA are outdated (the "zombie cases" mentioned above), you should tell your professor and also put it in the evaluation form at the end of the course. The beauty of the fractal world we live in is that patterns repeat, so most of the business phenomena that existed at the time of Standard Oil in the early twentieth century can be depicted by cases about Amazon and Google in the twenty-first century. Professors sometimes forget that "teaching young dogs old tricks" does not work as well as teaching young dogs "new tricks."

However, whatever the format and the content of the cases, there is no arguing that the discussions serve a valuable pedagogical purpose: they energize the class, which leads to enhanced learning. Just as atomic nuclei collide in a particle accelerator, MBA students clash in their case discussions, resulting in the release of energy in both situations.

3. Developing Hard Skills and Soft Skills

An MBA program is like a zipper: it brings together the left brain and the right brain, integrating soft skills and hard skills in a comprehensive educational experience. Hard skills are technical skills or knowledge: the skills required to do your basic job, e.g., data mining, marketing, accounting, and are gained primarily through education and training. On the other hand, soft skills (also known as human skills or people skills) are personal habits and traits, which define how you work with others or on your own. Soft skills are developed throughout life: critical thinking, problem-solving, creativity, adaptability, self-awareness, time management, teamwork, leadership, communication, and negotiation. As you can see from this list, many of the soft skills apply to how you manage yourself, not just how you interact with others.

Soft skills courses engender behavior change, which is one of the most elusive and notoriously hard things to achieve on your own. You probably know this already from your personal experience of trying and failing to change your behavior about something. Yet, there are techniques that have been perfected over decades by the leading researchers in soft skills areas and are applied by professors on willing-to-change students.

Sometimes students neglect some key soft skills courses (Ethical Leadership, Organizational Behavior, Human Resources Management, Effective Communication) because they are considered "lightweight," compared with Finance and Marketing, which can be applied directly in the job. However, polishing up your soft skills will support you throughout your career. Think about the MBA program as a building, with hard skills being the bricks and soft skills being the mortar that holds the bricks together. How long can a building made of bricks without mortar last in the wind and the rain?

Young people do tend to get hired in their first or second job based on hard skills: can you deliver what you are expected to do. This is because, at the bottom of the career ladder, you always start as an individual contributor. However, as you move up the hierarchy, you get evaluated more and more based on your soft skills: how you deal with and manage others. So in your very first job, it might be true that hard skills matter most while soft skills are merely a hygiene factor (a basic minimum threshold); whereas later in your career, the two get switched around: hard skills get downgraded to a hygiene factor (the bare minimum required), while soft skills shape your progression and promotions and ultimately define who you are within the organization.

All these observations can be put into a simple takeaway: Your soft skills make your hard skills shine!

4. Getting the Most Out of Your Professors

Before we tell you how to squeeze the maximum out of your professors, there are two important things you need to understand about academics in general. Both may sound counterintuitive:

First, our anecdotal evidence and observations show that many professors are introverts. Being introverted helps to complete a 3–5 year Ph.D. for a start (whereas many extroverts drop out of their Ph.D.) and to be able to focus on research and writing journal articles. This does not mean that such professors are poor communicators: it only means that communicating with people drains the energy of an introverted professor (whereas extroverts get recharged by communication). When teaching, introverted professors are usually able to "flip the switch" and act like an extrovert, but this would not be their normal or default state. So, an introverted professor needs time to recover their energy after a public event—they may go back to their office and may need to spend time on their own. So cut them some slack.

Second, research is the absolute priority for the vast majority of professors at all top business schools (i.e., at all research-intensive institutions). Professors get recognition and prestige in their subject area and among their international network of peers based on the research they publish in niche peer-reviewed journals. Teaching is important and nearly all have to do some teaching (rarely, some institutions may have research-only professors), but teaching is not the primary driver for a top professor. Teaching quality is merely a hygiene factor, so an "OK" student evaluation of a taught course ticks the teaching box and allows the professor to move on and focus on their research.

At lower-tier schools, professors are not expected to conduct as much research (and no research at all is expected at the very bottom of the business school rankings), so teaching remains the primary or only activity of professors at teaching-focused institutions. However, this does not necessarily translate into more focus on students at lower-tier schools, as a single professor at a teaching-only institution will be required to teach several times more class hours than at a research-intensive institution.

In the past, professors were the "fountain of knowledge" that students needed to drink from. Nowadays, there are many more fountains out there (especially online), so the usefulness of an MBA professor to students has shifted towards novel dimensions, which would not be expected or even suspected by the vast majority of students. We have three recommendations on how to benefit from developing a relationship with your professors:

First: identify possible mentors among your favorite professors. If you do well in a course, the professor will have more time for you outside of class. You can start building the relationship by talking to the professor about their Ph.D. dissertation and their current research. You can earnestly ask: "How can I learn from what you are working on and apply it in my future career?" You may get some interesting insights into the world of statistics and data analysis, the politics of gaining access to corporate data, etc. At a more practical level, if you receive multiple job offers, you could ask your mentor-professor which one to accept. And if you get along well, your professor may open up not only with advice but also with referrals and introductions.

Second: tap the professor's network. Many business school professors have moved beyond the "conveyor belt"/"factory mindset" view of teaching students at school (where the student is gone for good after graduation). A good business school professor will view their best students and graduates as a multi-generational community with which to keep in touch. Such professors are a "gold mine" of connections. We call it "a wheel of fortune": with the professor as the hub of this community and the alumni as the spokes. It is not uncommon for CEOs and HR directors who are graduates of an MBA program to go back to their professor when looking to fill a role and ask them to recommend current MBA students. And while most professors discourage "introduction" requests initiated by current students for fear of opening the floodgates to the entire class, the dynamics change once you graduate, and you can ask much more directly.

Third: do work for the professor and put it on your CV. Many professors need teaching assistants or research assistants. US schools in particular rely on assistants as a source of help and allocate a budget for them. Becoming a research/teaching assistant is a win–win, as this is a highly qualified part-time job. In a world where keywords are important, having an extra line on your CV improves your chances of getting your dream job. So why not ask your professor if they may have a job for you.

In return for everything that a professor may be able to do for you, you could repay their kindness by providing some qualitative feedback about their course. You would be surprised how little meaningful feedback students put in the evaluation forms at the end of a course, apart from the bare minimum of the numerical ratings (5 out of 5 points for content, 4 points for presentation, etc.). And even better, you can tell your professor in person what you liked in their course and what you struggled with, found not relevant, or disagreed with. Professors love an engaged student.

5. Integrative Courses and Final Project

We do not live in a siloed world: integration is the reality in all business and social activities. And rightly so, the business school curriculum tries to replicate the complexity of professional life with integrative courses and projects. Some subjects are more integrative than others by nature, for example, Strategy, Organizational Behavior, Business Ethics, and Sustainability have a lot more interconnections and linkages with other areas than Finance or Accounting. Furthermore, anything related to practice is likely to be integrative by definition, and business schools try to bring the curriculum closer to practice with dedicated courses such as Consultancy Skills and Management Practice, as well as with supervised internships/work placements.

The big integrative piece at the end of an MBA program is traditionally the master's thesis (known in the UK as a "dissertation") or more broadly a "final project." US MBA programs typically do not require a thesis but MBA programs in the US take longer on average, so they pack in more opportunities for integrative work during the semesters. In addition to the typical academic thesis/dissertation, the final project can also take the form of a Consultancy Report, a Startup Business Plan, or a Case Study on a company.

You have a lot of freedom in choosing the thesis/project topic, so use it judiciously. Think about your career 5–10 years into the future. You would want a topic/title that enhances your credibility in the given professional field : one that can be put on your CV and LinkedIn. Ideally, the topic of your final project should also be interesting to you, in addition to being beneficial to your career. And if you decide on the topic early on, you can collect materials for it throughout your studies.

A word of warning about thesis writing: be careful not to violate plagiarism rules in your write-up. Students from Asian cultures in particular struggle with plagiarism, as referencing is not taught at school early on. However, there is both a carrot and a stick connected with the use of citations. The "stick" part is the danger of getting a lower grade or completely failing your degree if significant plagiarism is proven (nowadays software such as Turnitin is widely used by schools to detect plagiarism, in particular in the MBA theses). The "carrot" end of the stick is that extensive referencing actually enhances the quality of your work and increases the chance of getting an excellent grade: it demonstrates that you have researched a lot of material and have selected a broad spectrum of sources (while also adding volume to your work).

At some schools, the thesis/final project is not merely submitted but also has to be "defended" with a live presentation, followed by a Q&A. The thesis defense is particularly important for projects that are prepared by a team of students, as it gives an opportunity to the judging panel to determine whether a given participant has contributed more or less to the joint team effort (so the grades of the team members from the thesis and/or the defense may differ).

6. Choosing Electives

Most MBA programs require students to take a number of elective courses, which typically come after the completion of the core courses. At some institutions, the electives are bundled into packages of courses from the same subject area that form specializations/concentrations/tracks. A student would usually be required to take three electives in the same field to gain a specialization. At smaller institutions, the range of electives may be more limited, and specialization bundles may not exist at all, allowing complete freedom to choose any of the electives on offer. You could even request to take an interesting course offered in other master's level programs at the business school or even at other schools within the university (e.g., in engineering or law), but you need to ask first—both for permission from the professor teaching the course and for assurance by your program director that the course will be recognized as an elective and count towards your MBA.

There may be some supply and demand dynamics around the systems of choosing electives. Some electives are always more popular than others, so schools may ration their supply by introducing a bidding system: each student is given 100 points, which they can allocate across their chosen electives. The successful bids will be the courses that attract the biggest number of points.

Seasoned MBA graduates recommend the following rule of thumb for making the decision about which courses to choose: "Take professors, not course titles!" The idea is that you would learn more from a great professor who is passionate about their subject than from an average professor who may be teaching an interesting-sounding course. There are two ways to find out who the best professors are: ask the students from the previous year for feedback; and audit the courses for a week before you make the decision (which is usually allowed at schools that offer a wide range of electives).

7. International Exchanges and Study Trips

An exchange semester is a great way for full-time MBA students to experience living in another country or even another continent. This is rarely an option for part-time MBA students unless they are willing to quit work for a semester and do the exchange in full-time mode. The PIM consortium[3] of 69 schools that facilitate exchange semesters amongst their members is just one of the possible avenues. There are also thousands of individual agreements between pairs of business schools to offer exchange semesters to their students on a reciprocal basis.

---

[3] PIM (n.d.).

It makes sense to try and do an exchange semester at a school that is seen as more prestigious than your own. This adds a couple of extra lines to your CV and gets you a foothold in a new alumni network (even though technically you will not be awarded alumni status, which is reserved only for those who complete a degree or a major executive education program). Schools within the PIM consortium generally want you to do your exchange semester abroad and would not allow an exchange at a school in the same country. Occasionally an MBA student may "trade down" and pick a less prestigious school than their own, but this should be done only if it is essential for your career or life plans (e.g., to get a foothold in Asia if you plan to move to Asia).

On the plus side of the networking balance sheet, doing an exchange semester can almost double your network of MBA classmates, acquaintances, and LinkedIn contacts. However, bear in mind that most of these will be "weak links" as you will not have much time to spend with them and develop a deeper relationship. On the minus side of the balance sheet, your original MBA class will keep bonding while you are away, so when you return to your "mother" school, you may find out that life has moved on and you are no longer as closely connected to your classmates as you were before you left. This applies most visibly to MBA programs where the class stays together as a cohort at least throughout the core courses; while it is not as much the case in programs that have staggered (carousel-model) entry points and the composition of the class keeps changing. Either way, both sides of the balance sheet bear out the saying: If you move around the world too much, you end up with many acquaintances and few friends.

Before making a decision on an exchange semester (typically 6 months before its start), make sure that it does not clash with your career plans and your job application timeline. If the on-campus job interviewing weeks overlap with your study-abroad plans, this may be a reason for doing a short 2-month exchange rather than a full semester exchange (which some PIM schools accommodate as well) or for going on a week-long study trip.

Study trips are fun as they combine learning opportunities in a new country with sightseeing, networking with external stakeholders, and bonding among students. The ratio between these components may vary, so check with previous cohorts if you care particularly one way or another. An international study trip is typically a week long and can be quite expensive (e.g., USD5000, not including the flights). Students who find the price tag difficult to afford usually have the choice to stay on campus and take an extra elective in the meantime.

8. Graduating On Time or Delaying Graduation

The writing of a thesis/final project sometimes results in a delay in graduation. Schools that require a thesis/project normally allocate a semester for it. Anything longer than a semester is tracked in the school's progression and completion system. Sometimes schools apply penalties (an additional fee or a thesis grade that is lower by default) to encourage students to graduate on time. It is not uncommon for students (luckily a small minority) to fail to graduate completely as a result of procrastinating and never completing/submitting their thesis.

Depending on the economic cycle, it may be judicious to request to stay on for an additional semester during a recession and graduate in a better economic climate (especially if you are studying full-time and applying for jobs). This may require paying an additional tuition fee but would also give you an opportunity to load up on all the electives that you may have missed.

Grades: A Non-issue

Grades are the one academic area that did not get its own number in this list. We did it for a reason. Adults care about grades a lot less than schoolchildren do; and your parents will not even know what grades you are getting. Grades are perhaps more important in a full-time MBA and matter less in a part-time MBA, but ultimately all MBAs are post-experience programs for mature adults who are not too bothered about their course grades. What matters is that the vast majority of MBA students who have been deemed worthy of admission and who put in the effort will manage to complete their courses.

There are just a couple of exceptions to the "grades do not matter" principle. For example, if you have a gap in your background, e.g., in quantitative subjects, and would like to move into a quantitatively-intensive career, it would be reassuring to potential employers to see in your transcript (and also reinforced in your CV and cover letter) that you have earned an excellent or above-average grade in the Statistics/Data Analysis or Quantitative Finance courses.

The other exception is if you did your MBA with company sponsorship or government sponsorship (some governments send their star civil servants abroad, with a 5-year contract of employment after returning from the MBA) and earning at least average or above-average grades is a condition of sponsorship.

To give you a bit of background, the grade in an MBA course is typically composed of several components: individual work/assignments; group project(s)/presentation(s); interim/final exams; and in-class participation. In group projects, peer evaluation is often a component of the grade: team members submit anonymously to the professor their evaluation for each fellow team participant to ensure that there are no free riders on the team. In-class participation is another interesting assessment rubric, sometimes with a weight of up to 30% of the course grade, as it encourages students to raise their hand and speak up. However, this is not a free-for-all opportunity to talk nonsense and professors will not hesitate to shut you up if your contributions to the class discussion are not valuable. In the long run, in team projects and class discussions, it probably matters more what impression you are leaving on your classmates than on the professor—you would not want to end up as the butt of all jokes among your classmates for the next decade or two.

Summary

The MBA resembles an academic retreat: it gives you the opportunity to walk out of the career "rat race" for a while and learn as much as possible in a compressed period of time. MBA students often talk about "epiphany," "Eureka," or "A-ha!" moments when they come to a fundamentally important realization, usually during a discussion in class or with classmates. The ones who love the MBA experience the most tend to be those MBA students who have completed their undergraduate studies a long time ago. The focus on practice, the case method and soft skills development, the freedom to choose electives, a final project, international exchanges and study trips, are all fundamentally different experiences not only from traditional university education but also from undergraduate business school education. So treat your MBA as both a privilege and as an obligation to deliver.

References

Banks, C. P. (2017). *The American legal profession: The myths and realities of practicing law*. SAGE.

Gloeckler, G. (2008, January 24). The case against case studies: How Columbia's B-school is teaching MBAs to make decisions based on incomplete data. *Bloomberg Businessweek*. Accessed April 23, 2023, from https://www.bloomberg.com/news/articles/2008-01-23/the-case-against-case-studies.

PIM. (n.d.). *PIM network*. Accessed April 26, 2023, from https://pim-network.org/.

7

How to Benefit Beyond the Academic Value of Your Business School and MBA Program

Introduction to Eight Non-academic Areas

Some marathon runners maintain that a marathon is an eating contest, not a running contest: whoever tops up their energy most efficiently wins. Business education cynics say something similarly counterintuitive: an MBA is a career contest, not a knowledge contest (it is not about what you learn, but where you end up on the career ladder). However, we strongly disagree with this adversarial black-and-white view of business education. The reality is a lot more nuanced: career success is based on a mix of many factors; and learning, knowledge, and skills are essential contributors. Below are some details and advice on eight (!) key non-academic themes to help you make the most of your time at business school.

1. Developing Self-Awareness via Personality Tests
All MBA programs start with an orientation, which lasts from 1 day to over a week. An important part of this orientation are personality/diagnostic tests that help you develop your self-awareness and understanding

of personality types (yours and those of others). The Myers–Briggs personality test focused on four dimensions (e.g., extraversion/introversion; thinking/feeling) used to be a staple of self-assessment testing, but has been dismissed in organizational behavior in recent years as scientifically flawed.[1] Instead, two other tests are widely used nowadays: The Big Five Personality Test (also known as OCEAN: openness, conscientiousness, extraversion, agreeableness, neuroticism) and the Belbin Team Role Inventories.

These tests help you find your bearings: understand better, who you are, what motivates and drives you, and how you interact with others. During your time at business school, this is particularly important for managing the many team projects that an MBA program requires. Chinese philosopher Laozi (the founder of Daoism/Taoism and author of "Daodejing") put it succinctly in his teachings 2500 years ago: 知人者智，自知者明 ("Those who understand others are clever, but those who know themselves are truly wise"). Self-awareness is the foundation of all soft skills development discussed earlier (communication, negotiation, leadership). The diagnostic tests will help you find out, among many other things, if you are a "dandelion" (a plant that grows anywhere) or an orchid (which requires certain conditions to thrive), i.e., an extrovert or an introvert, to borrow a metaphor from Susan Cain's book.[2]

Another useful tool in developing self-awareness is the Johari Window[3] framework of four combinations and intersections of what is known/unknown to others and what is known/unknown to self. The most interesting is the blind spot quadrant: what is known to others but not known to self. Blind spots can be illuminated through "360-degree" feedback exercises where you ask each of your teammates for qualitative feedback. This type of feedback can be painful but it would not be helpful if it were not critical (or else you would end up just tiptoeing around your blind spots). All personality and team diagnostic assessments exist for a reason: to help you in your career and future life.

---

[1] Schweiger (1985).
[2] Cain (2012).
[3] Francis (2020).

2. Extracurricular Activities (Events, Sports, Networking, Clubs)

Full-time MBA students are known to enjoy all the opportunities that life on campus brings: from networking events with MBA alumni, students from other schools, or corporate executives; to drinking parties (sometimes supported or encouraged by the school itself in the form of "Thursday afternoon kegs" on campus) and pub crawls; to sports activities (golf, football, etc.), games (paintball) and extreme sports such as tandem parachute jumps. Western schools (in America and Europe) generally tend to promote activities that suit extroverted behavior, while Asian schools tone down the extroversion a bit. However, drinking in China and Japan appears to be on par with and as important as drinking in the West—perhaps only the style is different.

Student clubs/societies are important to get involved in for not only the content of the events they put on and the networking opportunities, but also for the availability of leadership positions. A club/society will typically have at least a President and one Vice President and there could be several dozen clubs at your school, so if you run for a few leadership roles, you are likely to get at least one or two positions to put on your CV. This can be important, particularly for students who want to change careers: getting into a leadership role at a club relevant to your future industry will add a few important keywords to your story and proof of your commitment.

Universities often have amazing campuses with fancy facilities. Access to the university sports center is typically covered by the tuition fee package, so given that you will already be paying for the sports center, why not use the swimming pool and the gym.

In 2022, Columbia Business School unveiled in New York City its new USD600 million building—the most expensive business school building ever constructed. The idea behind such fancy buildings is that they create an ecosystem of activities and a hub that draws people together. The irony is on-campus facilities are primarily used by current students, even though alumni may have unrestricted access to the events and activities. Unless working alumni are individually invited (e.g., as event speakers), even if they are based in the same city, they will typically stop by on campus only a couple of times a year.

Part-time MBA students generally do not have as much time as full-time MBAs to stay on campus before/after their classes and any scheduled teamwork activities, so they get less involved in all things extracurricular.

3. Utilizing the Career Centre

The MBA degree is sometimes confused with the NBA (the National Basketball Association in the US) because of the similarity of the two acronyms. This superficial similarity aside, there is one aspect of the MBA that bears a striking resemblance to a spectacular feature of American basketball: the slam dunk. A basketball player performs a slam-dunk by jumping high in the air and shoving the ball into the basket with great force. Similarly, an MBA student dives into the MBA experience and expects to land a great job in the end. However, just as many shots in basketball do not lead to scoring a point, not every single MBA student manages to score a career "slam dunk." How MBAs engage with their school's Career Centre can make all the difference.

Work with the Career Centre starts from Day 1 of the program (and if it does not, there must be something wrong with the MBA program you have enrolled in). Career development, CV writing, and job interviewing training and exercises delivered by the Career Centre are often part of the official curriculum even if typically they are non-graded, or they can be run as extracurricular activities. The formal training is followed by one-on-one or group coaching, mock interviews, and simulations with an appointed career advisor. The objective is to get you a job as high as possible on the career ladder (if you are a full-time student) or to earn you a promotion (if studying part-time). Recording videos of yourself is the norm as part of the interview preparation exercises, as it helps to get comfortable with how you appear on camera.

Sometimes schools mistakenly refuse to provide Career Centre services to company-sponsored employees on the assumption that this category of MBA students do not need to look for a job, or even on the mistaken understanding that it would be unethical to open up opportunities for other companies to "poach" an employee who has company sponsorship. AMBA recommends that schools should always offer Career Development training to all MBA students. While schools do need to withhold outright job placement services from company-sponsored students, Career Development is a much broader category that also includes advancing within the company, negotiating promotions, managing upwards, developing board relations, etc., so it complements the soft skills development of the individual.

Job placement of full-time MBA students is a key performance indicator for the appointed career advisor. Career Centre staff may even be financially incentivized (as a bonus or percentage of their remuneration) if they manage to hit employment targets, e.g., helping over 95% of the job-seekers in the MBA class to get a job within 3 months of graduation. So if you receive a suboptimal job offer and your adviser recommends accepting it, bear in mind that they may be doing it partly to hit their own target…so feel free to push back and make your own decision.

An unfortunate side effect of the support role of a Career Centre is that students use it as a ladder to climb up the corporate hierarchy and then discard the ladder when it is no longer needed (if Austrian philosopher Ludwig Wittgenstein would allow us to borrow his metaphor). When students land their dream job, they usually celebrate it as their own success. While if they fail to get a job, they often blame the Career Centre for not having helped them enough. As a result, even the best Career Centers often get bad publicity among the student/alumni network, so do not worry unnecessarily about the reputation of your Career Centre: there will always be below-average performers among the students (the worst are known as "the squeaky wheels").

Autonomous Career Centers that are nested at the business school (and whose staff report to the school dean) traditionally do a better job of offering quality career support and job placement than a Career Centre whose home and line of responsibility is the university at large (a model known as "shared services"). MBA students need more sophisticated support, while university-nested career support is primarily geared towards the undergraduate level to service large numbers of junior job seekers, which results in a possible mismatch. The autonomy, structure, and reporting lines of the Career Centre would be an excellent topic to explore during your MBA admissions interview.

In the long run, your Career Centre is supposed to support you for life in your career endeavors. We say "supposed to" because if you no longer live in the same city, the help you can get far away or abroad is limited. Also, you are likely to outgrow the level of services that the Career Centre provides once you have your own robust professional network firmly established. Yet, once in a while, the Career Centre may be of some help—so do not discard it completely even after 20 years from graduation.

4. Company Visits

"Field trips" is another name for company visits, which also combine talks/presentations on company premises. These are one of the distinctive features of management education, focused on showcasing practice in the environment of the practitioners.

Company visits are a favorite activity for MBA students because they require little preparation but can be interesting not just for the content of the presentations by a company executive but also for the trail of discovery during the tour of the company. They also offer potential leads to employment opportunities: ask an insightful question to a senior executive and you have your foot in the door that can turn into a follow-up coffee chat and then into an internship or a job interview.

Company visits are also distinctly memorable parts of the MBA and there is a biological reason for this. There are at least three different types of neurons that encode the memory of location in the human brain (a discovery that won the 2014 Nobel Prize in physiology and medicine), so when students are taken out of the business school environment, this creates very strong new memories based on the novel locations.

5. Informational Interviews

An informational interview is an informal chat with an executive (typically an alum of your school or an MBA alum from elsewhere) initiated by the MBA student. It has two objectives: to allow the student to learn more about the company where the executive is working; and to send a strong signal to the executive that the student is interested in the company. Therefore, you should always come to an informational interview prepared, having reviewed in advance the publicly available information about the company (company website, Wikipedia page, recently published online articles), so that you can ask insightful questions that only the executive can answer, i.e., a level above the generic information that is in the public domain.

Culturally, US MBA students are the most attuned to this format as it is an established practice in American corporate life. European MBA students—less so, and most East Asian students would not even dare chat up/message an executive they do not know. However, all MBAs should do this, irrespective of their location, as these types of meetings are the entryway to the MBA job market. So do not hesitate to pursue managers, directors, vice presidents, and even CEOs with polite requests for informational interviews. In the worst case, they will say "No."

Once an executive has accepted, events may force them to postpone or reschedule an agreed meeting. That should not surprise you: the power lies with the busy executive who does not have much to gain from such a meeting with a supplicant MBA student. In such a case, respond politely and simply reschedule. You should only consider abandoning the plan to meet with someone who has previously agreed to talk to you if they cancel three times.

A psychological trick (taught by Organizational Behavior professors) to increase your chances of getting a meeting scheduled in the first place is to ask for an interview 3 weeks into the future, when the agenda of the busy executive is not entirely packed and the discounting of future time works in your favor. We humans view as a more constrained resource the immediate future and are more relaxed about the more distant future, so it is easier to get a commitment to a meeting weeks away.

6. Formal Job/Internship Interviews

Companies nowadays use rounds of interviews, sometimes resorting to as many as a dozen different interviewers. This is in line with diversity principles but also out of necessity—to give the hiring managers a sneak preview of their potential employees. Reporting lines at a matrix-structured organization can be fuzzy, so several managers may have interactions with the position they are trying to fill.

In order to come across as competent and confident, you need to rehearse answering interview-type questions. To prepare, ask a friend or a classmate to run a mock interview with you and ideally record you on video, so you can watch it later. Conducting the mock interview on Zoom would make recording even easier. If you do not have anyone at hand, rehearse in front of the mirror or on your phone in video recording format.

Knowing your CV well is the first step to a successful interview. Consultancies such as McKinsey employ an interviewing technique where they pick one of your past employment periods and drill deeper and deeper until they have exhausted every possible question. This reveals how you perform under pressure but also helps them expose people who have "doctored" their CVs with non-existent titles and job content.

The second part of the interview is usually about storytelling: "Tell me about a time when …" Normally a dozen types of situations are commonly called for, inviting you to demonstrate your leadership, perseverance, etc. However, preparing just five or six good stories can cover a plethora of different situations. If you have a story about a time when you had to fire an employee, this would not only be a story about firing people; it could also be a story about leadership, operational excellence, overcoming obstacles, showing empathy, etc. And even if you do not have the perfect story on the requested topic, tell the interviewer your most closely related story and ask at the end: "Did I answer your question with this?" Usually, the interviewer will waive you on, rather than risk getting bogged down for 10 more minutes on the same topic.

Good preparation also requires rehearsing your stories with a simplified storyline and with details pared down to the minimum (at least initially). Applying the STAR storytelling technique (situation-task-action-result) can help you boil down every story into just four sentences. Remember: your interviewer not only does not care about the minutiae of the story but could also end up confused and lose the thread if you give them too many unnecessary details.

Interviewers leave the last 5–10 min for you to ask them questions. Always prepare a few relevant questions about the company, department, and role. And if you are ever taken by surprise, even generic questions about the person will do the job: "What is the hardest part of your job?" "Does your role leave you time for your hobbies?" We are all humans, so harking back to the humanity of the person will create a feeling of proximity with them.

If you are lucky to receive multiple job offers, you may have some difficult decisions to make. What makes things even more difficult are mutually-exclusive timelines: you may have a job offer from your second most desirable company that expires days before you will find out if the company of your top choice will make you an offer. Career Centers remind students to be ethical and stick to commitments once a job offer has been accepted. Yet, having options is clearly preferable to not having any options at all, so do as many interviews as you get invited to.

7. Mentoring

Most leading MBA programs have an institutionalized mentoring scheme that pairs up an alum of the school with a current MBA student. Mentoring is a two-way street: you get mentored by people who are more senior and experienced than you, but at the same time you should be prepared to mentor those who are younger and less experienced than you, to "pay forward" (e.g., bachelor students at your school). Mentoring is also a two-way street in another sense: you are learning both when being mentored and when mentoring (e.g., learning about yourself or learning about new technologies from your younger mentee, etc.).

Ideally, your mentor should not be your direct manager at your company. This prevents conflicts of interest and helps you broaden your network. The V-formation of wild geese in flight is a good analogy for mentoring schemes: the goose in front helps the goose behind it by reducing the air resistance and creating an uplift, which is why birds often fly in a V-formation. The best spot following the front goose is not immediately behind it but slightly sideways (to minimize air turbulence); just as with the advice we give about avoiding a mentor from your company who is positioned immediately above you.

8. Prioritizing

Setting priorities is an essential part of strategy. Strategic thinking and strategic planning are often about what you say "No" to, as much as what you say "Yes" to. At INSEAD, MBA students talk about the "3S" dilemma: during your MBA you will have time for only two of the three "S": sleep, study, socialize. We have added a fourth "S" to this principle: search (job search), so analogously, this would require MBA students to pick three out of the four "S." Whatever the number, you get the idea: time is the most precious resource.

US schools send their full-time MBA students to career fairs as early as September in their first year, in order to prepare them for the summer internship interviews that take place in/around January. And even if January is also the month of exams, when a key internship/job interview is at stake, studying takes the back seat.

The list of trade-offs may contain many other difficult decisions that require prioritizing one over the other:

- If you did not receive a job offer after your summer internship, perhaps you have to reconsider doing that fun exchange semester on the other side of the world (if you will not be applying for jobs in that region).
- If you do not have a job offer near the time of your graduation, you may want to ask your school to enroll you in an extra elective or two, or in an additional semester—to allow you to continue your job search while officially still being part of the MBA (rather than apply for jobs as an unemployed graduate about whom employers will wonder what went wrong).
- Re-evaluate which two parts of the "Triple Jump" in your job search you may want to keep or give up (changing country, changing industry, or changing function).
- Consider as a backup option the "Bungee Jump": going back to your previous employer or to your country of origin if your other job search scenarios fail.
- If your dream job offer has not materialized, go down the list of other backup options: if investment banking is a "No," perhaps a job in corporate finance will be easier to land.

Summary

The better you prepare for the MBA in advance, the more you will get out of it. However, do not rush through the MBA and expect every piece of knowledge and experience to fall into its place immediately. You will only appreciate the true value of some of your experiences, takeaways, and encounters years after graduation.

Appreciating the complexity of the modern world, a Communications Professor from a leading business school used to say that "no one really knows what they are doing." And after observing how strategic planning is done in various sectors, we can attest to this. So, enjoy the organized chaos that the MBA brings into your life and make the most of it.

References

Cain, S. (2012). *Quiet: The power of introverts in a world that can't stop talking.* Crown Publishing Group.

Francis, N. (2020, February 10). The importance of self-awareness for effective leadership. *CEO World Magazine.* Accessed April 23, 2023, from https://ceoworld.biz/2020/02/10/the-importance-of-self-awareness-for-effective-leadership/.

Schweiger, D. M. (1985). Measuring managerial cognitive styles: On the logical validity of the Myers-Briggs Type Indicator. *Journal of Business Research, 13*(4), 315–328.

Part III

Benefiting from the Long-Term Value of Your MBA

8

How an MBA Can Boost Your Career

Life may be a box of chocolates (to borrow Forrest Gump's metaphor) but an MBA is a lot more cohesive than this: it is a stew in which the ingredients blend in and reinforce each other. Opting for an MBA equips you with a lasting source of motivation and determination to excel in your career. Your career is the project of a lifetime and the MBA is one of the best ways to lay a solid professional foundation for it.

Two key reasons why MBA graduates are successful in their careers are contained in the two important steps that precede starting an MBA: your subjective self-selection (your own decision to explore what an MBA means, including your self-evaluation that you are good enough to do it), followed by the rigorous and more objective selection by the school's admissions team. Only the more driven amongst us will self-select to do an MBA and this is an important starting point that differentiates the minority of would-be MBAs from the majority of people who will never do an MBA. Then the selection process further reduces the size of this select club, just as a "reduction" in cooking reduces the volume of the sauce, concentrates the ingredients, and intensifies the flavor. Thus, the MBA becomes a self-fulfilling prophecy: if you have started one, you have already signaled to yourself and to the world that you are ready to succeed in business and in life.

Below are the eight key components that we believe uniquely position the MBA as a lifelong career booster.

1. Opportunity to Step Up or Change Direction

There are competing metaphors that describe the unique opportunity that the MBA creates for you to change direction or make the next step up the ladder. We are laying out three of these metaphors below, not aiming to overwhelm you but rather to drive home the message that this only happens once in a lifetime.

- Most careers are linear: like driving on a motorway/highway with very few exits, spaced far apart. On the other hand, the MBA creates a roundabout/traffic circle (USA) from which you can leave in multiple directions. In the long run, the MBA also helps lay out more roundabouts along your career trajectory by helping you develop a somewhat "opportunistic" (in a positive sense) view of the world. Appreciating the volatile, uncertain, complex, and ambiguous (VUCA) world we live in, some cutting-edge MBA programs (e.g., at IE Business School, Madrid) teach "strategic opportunism" as the winning career strategy: you should roughly know the direction in which you want to develop, but always keep your options open in case an opportunity that is tangential to your predetermined direction comes knocking on your door. In entrepreneurship, this type of changing direction is called a "strategic pivot." Successful startups often need to perform several strategic pivots until they find their market niche and achieve product-market fit. And you, too, can view your career as the startup of a lifetime and keep your options open to iterate and change direction at every roundabout along the motorway of life.
- Continuing the theme of moving at high speed, Formula 1 cars go into a pit stop to change their worn-out tires. The MBA creates a similar opportunity to revisit your career goals and to change trajectory if you decide to throw out the worn-out tires and switch gears (i.e., careers).

2. Confidence Booster

The MBA helps you build up two types of confidence and these can make a huge difference in your career: the courage to speak up and stand out, and the openness and willingness to compare yourself against others. The MBA not only makes you more visible to the world by integrating you into various executive networks; it also helps you gain visibility into the business world and a better understanding of what other people's careers look like. The MBA makes you comfortable with visibility and teaches you how to leverage visibility to achieve the maximum impact in your career: it polishes up your self-selected strengths and enhances your confidence to stand out and be seen and heard.

Bertrand Russell said: "Do not fear to be eccentric in opinion, for every opinion now accepted was once eccentric."[1] MBA students and graduates are often ridiculed for their overweening self-confidence, along the lines that "The mark of a true MBA is that he is often wrong, but seldom in doubt", according to Harvard professor Robert Buzzell (Note that it is more often a "he" than a "she"). However, MBA programs actually teach a much more nuanced and benevolent approach to confidence: "Speak like you are right; listen like you are wrong."—i.e., project the image of a steadfast executive who makes firm decisions, while actually taking feedback on board and keeping an open mind, including the possibility to change your mind.

Some MBA professors teach a range of simple psychological tricks to boost your self-confidence when you need it the most. For example, when you go for a job interview, arrive early but keep walking around the building so that you enter the meeting room minutes before the start and thus carry some of your physical momentum into the conversation. And when talking, stand with your chest out and avoid crossing your hands in a supplicant position in order to boost your confidence.[2]

One of the key differences between an academic master's degree and an MBA is where the two aim to position you on the thought versus action continuum. While both develop your analytical skills and help you become a better "thought leader," the MBA goes the extra step and pushes

---

[1] Russell (n.d.).
[2] Ohio State University (2009).

you to adopt a default frame of mind where you want to take action after performing the analysis (as opposed to inaction resulting from "analysis-paralysis"). Therefore, the MBA aims to create not just thought leaders but action leaders.

Confidence also means the courage to compare yourself with others as objectively as you can, so that you can benchmark against their skills and achievements and learn from them. The most helpful framework for this is described by the Dunning–Kruger effect:[3] above-average people tend to overestimate others, while below-average people overestimate themselves. And here is the crucial twist once you have learned about the existence of Dunning–Kruger in your Organizational Behavior class: people with below-average abilities are boastful, so to distance yourself from them you have to counter-signal (i.e., to do the opposite).

3. Eight MBA Learning Outcomes

Every good MBA program defines a set of learning outcomes that students must achieve by the time they graduate. These may sound a bit abstract (and are rarely even shown to students by the program directors) but they define the strategic priorities of the program. Learning outcomes at the undergraduate level are primarily about knowing facts and theories; in higher-level programs, the outcomes are increasingly centered on skills and competencies, with values and attitudes added to the mix. These key learning outcomes are the stepping stones on which you build your career. Below are the eight that feature most frequently in the leading MBA programs around the world:

Critical thinking Critical thinking is the questioning/challenging approach to processing information and making decisions. Its key constituent is the ability to identify and challenge assumptions (unspoken conclusions): a crucial skill that is universally useful, from office communication to high-level boardroom discussions. The course in Organizational Behavior is particularly conducive to developing this skill as its focus on

---
[3] Dunning (2011).

interpersonal and cultural differences highlights how differently we perceive the world. The "Analysis of an Argument" part of the GMAT test is an exercise focused specifically on identifying assumptions, so by taking the GMAT you get to practice this even before starting your MBA.

Global mindset Even local MBA programs taught in a local language aim to develop a global mindset in their students: through international case studies, simulations, study trips, guest speakers, etc. If you keep a list of all the case studies you have done in your MBA, you could impress even the most skeptical recruiter.

Strategic thinking Not all problems require strategic thinking. Some problems can be dealt with by simply following a predetermined recipe/algorithm of actions (or by falling back on habits in everyday life). Others can be solved by benchmarking against existing practice elsewhere (copycatting). However, higher-order complex challenges require strategic thinking, which Henry Mintzberg defines as more about synthesis ("connecting the dots") than analysis ("finding the dots").[4]

MBA programs teach you at the most practical level how to create the right conditions for strategic thinking: by periodically cutting yourself off from mundane everyday tasks and going on a retreat, or simply by switching off all devices for a day in order to minimize disruptions and thus reach a state of "flow." This resembles the way green pastures for grazing animals are revived: you have to close off the plot to let it recover from the hooves that have trampled on it.

Entrepreneurial spirit London Business School compares entrepreneurship in the MBA with the swimming pool of a social club: different people use it for different purposes, from splashing around to doing fast-paced laps. Similarly, some MBA students develop their own startups (which may evolve into scaleups and the occasional unicorn), while oth-

---

[4] Mintzberg (1994).

ers apply principles of entrepreneurship and innovation in their corporate career (e.g., the "Lean Startup" principles developed by Eric Ries).[5]

Another set of metaphors captures the advantages of an entrepreneurial spirit: While a corporate career resembles the controlled flight of a plane (with the departure runway, cruising route, and landing airport all being fixed as planned), an entrepreneurial venture resembles the flight of a bird (which can take off from anywhere, fly freely, and land on anything). These analogies are reinforced by a reminder to any corporate executive who falls on hard times (when their plane starts to "break down") that they can hit the eject button and turn into a bird mid-flight by launching their own startup.

Collaborative leadership and teamwork Teaching leadership is like a plane seeding the clouds to produce artificial rain: if there is humidity in the atmosphere, the intervention can turn into rainmaking and the streaks of rainwater would grow into a mighty river. Similarly, once you have had some leadership experiences in your pre-MBA life, a leadership professor helps you coalesce these through self-reflection and channel them into enhancing your ability to lead organizations.

An MBA program also develops a practical appreciation for teamwork and flat organization through the multiple group projects that students engage in.

Effective communication Several of the key lifelong communication skills that an MBA develops include:

Appreciation for small talk as a social lubricant at all levels, including as a key component in projecting senior presence in Western cultures

- The STAR/SOAR storytelling methods (referred to in Chap. 5), condensing any plot into four sentences
- The ability to structure information by distilling it into executive summaries, concise email subject lines, numbered lists (preferable to bullet points), and visualization tools such as metaphors and memes that capture the essence of a situation

---

[5] Ries (2011).

- Presentation skills, including how to manage your stage presence
- The ability to pass the "airport test" that comes from the consulting sector: if you were stranded at an airport with a colleague, would you be able to find enough interesting topics to talk about while waiting for the next flight 6 h later?

Negotiation An MBA gives you a set of tools to use in negotiations, e.g., the skill to signal a strong BATNA (best alternative to a negotiated solution) without ever revealing your "reservation price" (the point at which you walk away). However, even more importantly, the MBA leaves you with two key conceptual takeaways:

- Everything in life is negotiable to some degree, so once you know this and you have the confidence, you can engage in these negotiations, whether you are negotiating a pay rise with your boss or with an interviewing panel the terms of a CEO role.
- Success in a negotiation is correlated with the time you invest in preparation for it. Therefore, no matter what tools and frameworks you may use in advance, if you prepare and think about the issues up-front, the investment of time will pay off.

Ethical decision-making and sustainability Most good MBA programs teach ethics and sustainability almost imperceptibly: not in the form of a stand-alone course but by infusing all courses, projects, and activities with ethical angles and sustainability elements. Beyond that, a good professor will reinforce the learnings through repetition of the key points. By the end of the MBA program, you should feel confident that you have a sufficient understanding of business ethics to stand the test that Benjamin Franklin once put in a quote: "It is hard for an empty sack to stand upright."[6] A key takeaway from business ethics comes in the form of a warning: "do not do something if you would not like to see it printed on the front page of your local newspaper."

---

[6] Franklin (n.d.).

As you can see from the brief description of these eight learning outcomes, they form a solid foundation for a solid career.

4. Toolkit of Frameworks

Socrates compared the human mind to an aviary where every piece of knowledge is a different bird. He did note a complication though: even if you are the owner of this aviary, the birds do not always land on your shoulder when you ask them to. Analogously, education gives you knowledge but the MBA goes a step further and gives you practical tools and frameworks that are easy to recall and apply in your career. These frameworks are the birds that (almost) always land on your shoulder when you need them.

The "2×2" matrix is the workhorse of business education and the corporate world.[7] Most challenges can be conceptualized and boiled down to the interplay of two factors, which produces four strategies in the four quadrants, respectively. There are hundreds of useful matrices and you may start accumulating your own set of favorites. As just one example, almost all companies use the Growth-Share Matrix (also known as the BCG Matrix)[8] which positions a company's products into four categories: question marks (high growth, low market share); stars (high growth, high share); cash cows (low growth, high share); and dogs (low growth, low share).

Delving into the workings of the mind, the MBA exposes you to a range of behavioral (cognitive) biases that help you better understand your friends and family, colleagues and competitors, but also yourself. An inventory of 188 cognitive biases lists the main ones.[9] For example: anchoring bias (you tend to get anchored on the first piece of information you see), availability heuristic (relying on what you can recall to explain the world), or the wonderful Pygmalion effect (you perform better when someone has high expectations of you).

The simplest thinking concept of all is benchmarking: look around to see what other companies and people are doing and try it out yourself, instead of trying to "reinvent the wheel" every time. Bismarck said, "Only

---

[7] McDonald and Leppard (1993).
[8] BCG (n.d.).
[9] Desjardins (2021).

a fool learns from his own mistakes. The wise man learns from the mistakes of others."[10] This makes perfect sense for anyone even without an MBA, but your MBA will further reinforce this message with two political heuristics: If you copy a successful strategy from your competitor and it does not work out, you are less likely to be blamed (or fired) than if you developed a strategy entirely on your own. And to distance yourself further from the fallout of failure, you can hire a consulting firm to do the benchmarking for you and to recommend the path to take. There is a saying in the business world that no one ever gets fired for hiring McKinsey (if you can afford it). So, if a strategy does not work out, you blame the consultants for it (which, anecdotally, is one of the accepted reasons why consultants exist in the first place: to take the blame for failure).

All these frameworks are mental shortcuts: thinking tools and decision-making models that will serve you throughout your career. And if your personal inventory (collection) of such frameworks is on your phone or in the cloud, you always have them at hand and are never at risk of the bird in the aviary not landing on your shoulder.

5. Global Hub for Your Career

An MBA creates not just one but three global hubs for your career: the business school career center, the business school at large, and the university at large (if the school is part of a university). All three can support you in different ways. The career center has the responsibility to assist you with introductions and referrals (although after graduation you are less of a priority for them than the current students); the business school runs events that you can tap into, in addition to your network of professors who can also make introductions and bring you job opportunities; and the university events, even if not as closely targeted at the corporate level, can lead to beneficial chance encounters.

Business schools have many similarities with social clubs (London-style) and country clubs (US-style): they are places for people to meet and network. However, you should always remember that the gravitational

---

[10] Von Bismarck (n.d.).

pull of your business school is strongest in the city where it is based, because of all the connections and the concentration of alumni, employers, and professors. And if it happens that your school is based in a global city, so much the better for your career as you are more likely to end up working at corporate headquarters. Careers get accelerated at headquarters more naturally because of the physical proximity to the decision-making processes, the key people, and even the chance conversations at the watercooler, which can (even by chance) open up paths to promotion and opportunities to lead.

6. Support from Alumni Networks

Given the importance of alumni, we have dedicated a special chapter on this topic, but here we give you a couple of glimpses from a historical and geographical perspective. The Association of MBAs (AMBA) was founded in London in 1967 as a global club for MBA alumni. Before the Internet age, it used to print a directory booklet with all members' contact details grouped by school, city, and industry annually. The world does not need such a booklet anymore as LinkedIn and various other platforms serve as an easily accessible directory. However, this demonstrates a key point: MBA networks exist across the world in various fuzzy formats, just as the underground mycelium structures of fungus connect the roots of trees and provide nutrition to them. At some schools, these networks are not even fuzzy and informal: the leading business school in Madrid, IE (Instituto de Empresa), has official representatives/country managers in some 30 key cities around the world who deal with alumni relations (as well as support recruiting) in their territory.

The MBA also teaches you how to make the most of the alumni network: by actively reaching out and inviting those relevant to your career plans to coffee or lunch; by exploring common ground that can create proximity between you; by asking for mentorship, etc. A great strategy to stay close to key alumni is to join all types of school boards that you can get into: the Alumni Committee, Advisory Board, Board of Trustees (and not only those of your own alma mater but of other institutions as well).

7. Lifelong Learning Platform

By giving you a solid foundation in over a dozen subject areas and showing you the speed of change and creation of new knowledge in these fields, the MBA prepares you for a lifetime of learning. This is crucial in today's job market where many of the jobs did not exist until recently (Hello, Instagram influencers!). Some experts take issue with the term "lifelong learning" and prefer to call it "lifestyle learning" to better reflect the ease with which it can be integrated into working life and family life. Aalto Business School in Finland (known for design and design thinking in particular) even calls its offering "lifewide learning" to highlight the different settings in which the learning process takes place. Either way, the message is clear: whatever the format and the word for it, lifelong learning is crucial for your career development.

Massive online open courses (MOOC) saw phenomenal growth on platforms such as Coursera in the mid-2010s, while stackable certificates (courses that you get credit for) have been growing at business schools since the start of the Covid-19 pandemic. Both of these are part of the lifelong learning movement, though MBA graduates care more about the flexibility and ease of access than the academic credits that go with it. We too are advocates for these flexible modes of delivery, including even the possibility of designing MBA programs that are composed of a set of stackable certificates (which is still some way into the future). Taking this and stretching it out in time, a novel idea called "degrees for rent" allows for MBA programs to be designed as an initial intensive period of learning, followed by electives spread out over years or decades, with a mandatory requirement to top up with a new course every once in a while in order to maintain your MBA degree status (described by one of the book's authors in an interview with the Financial Times).[11] This idea exposes the drawbacks of the current situation (a degree up-front and no follow-up topping up or updating required).

On a practical level, as soon as you graduate, you need to check if your school offers any MBA electives to alumni for free or for a small fee. Schools often do this to maintain the connection with alumni, unless they have a significant Executive Education offering and fear that free or

---

[11] Moules (2019).

cheap electives may undermine the demand for expensive Exec Ed courses. On the other hand, some schools treat the MBA electives as tasters for the Exec Ed portfolio, so it is worth checking. Alumni also tend to like joining the international study trips organized for current MBA students and some schools welcome alumni participation in these (especially if the group of current students is not too big).

One last piece of practical advice: keep your MBA lecture notes and do not let your partner/husband/wife throw them away (we are speaking from experience here). Their content may get obsolete in 20 years but this is exactly the point—to create a point of comparison and a reminder of where you started and how far you have come over two decades.

Lifelong learning is a philosophy of staying (metaphorically) hungry, along the lines of Steve Jobs' famous quote "Stay hungry! Stay foolish!"[12] In a way, this philosophy resembles the story of co-dependent evolution between humans and shepherd dogs: humans have selectively bred dogs such as Labradors over millennia so that they evolved to always be hungry and thus be obedient servants to the human (who would feed them a tasty morsel in exchange for performing a work task). In a similar way, the job market has made all of us "hungry learners," as we would fall by the wayside and become less employable if we stopped learning.

We end this topic with one last metaphor: lifelong learning is like popping popcorn in the microwave oven. Just as some students are keener or faster learners than others, in the microwave oven of lifelong learning some of the corn may pop sooner and some may take longer. However, everybody is equipped to be a lifelong learner: you just need to keep the corn in the microwave long enough and eventually, it will all turn into popcorn.

8. Leaving a Legacy

Jack Ma, the founder of Alibaba, advises young graduates to keep shifting their focus during a 40-year career:[13] In your 20s: join a good company and learn; in your 30s: experiment with your own projects (startups); in

---

[12] Jobs (2005).
[13] Mejia (2018).

your 40s: double down on your strengths and do what you are good at; and in your 50s: think about your legacy by helping the next generation of young people.

We do not have data on how MBAs in particular perform along this sequence of stages but 2019 research shows that American university-educated women see their earnings peak at age 44 and US men with university degrees reach their peak earning power at age 55.[14] The gender disparity aside, what is also important is that even though people may peak in their career in terms of position in the corporate hierarchy and earnings potential, they do not necessarily peak at the same time in their real-world impact. This is also borne out by Jack Ma's advice about your career in your 50s: leveraging the previous three decades, you can maximize your impact in society by helping others in their careers and thus leave your mark on the world. In marathon running, there is an interesting analogy: some professional runners complete the second half of the marathon faster than the first half (an intentional strategy known as "negative split"). With this metaphor for impact in mind, it is inspirational to ponder if the second half of your life can be more impactful on the world than the first half.

There is an additional angle to this story. Everybody who has completed a leading MBA program has benefited enormously from the generosity and kindness of others: through advice, support, and mentorship. So parallel to being thankful to the people who have supported you ("paying back"), you should "pay forward" and offer the same support to the younger generations. This strategy is philanthropic but is not entirely selfless: your later career can get an unexpected boost if you are seen by the most senior people in your organization to be engaging with society and doing good.

Summary

We talk about the MBA as a once-in-a-lifetime opportunity to discover new horizons and re-energize your career. In this sense, an MBA is forever, just like "diamonds are forever." The similarities between MBAs and

---

[14] Perez (2019).

diamonds do not end here. We discussed the key role of self-selection at the beginning of this chapter: if you are going for an MBA, you are already a precious stone, a raw diamond. What the MBA accomplishes is cutting the surface of the diamond by creating hundreds of facets and polishing it to give it maximum brilliance. Just like a diamond that has been cut, a person who has completed an MBA becomes more valuable on the market.

We leave you with one last analogy between MBAs and diamonds: diamonds are brilliant because they reflect light at many different angles; and MBAs use their accomplished skills and privileged position not only to advance their own interests but also to help others achieve remarkable things in their diverse careers.

References

BCG. (n.d.). What is the growth share matrix? *BCG*. Accessed April 23, 2023, from https://www.bcg.com/about/overview/our-history/growth-share-matrix.

Desjardins, J. (2021, August 26). Every single cognitive bias in one infographic. *VisualCapitalist*. Accessed March 12, 2023, from https://www.visualcapitalist.com/every-single-cognitive-bias/.

Dunning, D. (2011). The Dunning–Kruger effect: On being ignorant of one's own ignorance. *Advances in experimental social psychology, 44*, 247–296.

Franklin, B. (n.d.). Benjamin Franklin quotes. *Goodreads*. Accessed April 23, 2023, from https://www.goodreads.com/quotes/890653-it-is-hard-for-an-empty-sack-to-stand-upright.

Jobs, S. (2005, June 12). Steve Jobs' 2005 Stanford commencement address. [Video]. *Youtube*. Accessed May 15, 2023, from https://www.youtube.com/watch?v=UF8uR6Z6KLc&t=830s.

McDonald, M., & Leppard, J. (1993). *Marketing by matrix: 100 practical ways to improve your strategic and tactical marketing*. NTC Business Book.

Mejia, Z. (2018, January 30). Self-made billionaire Jack Ma: How to be successful in your 20s, 30s, 40s and beyond. *CNBC*. Accessed April 12, 2023, from https://www.cnbc.com/2018/01/30/jack-ma-dont-fear-making-mistakes-in-your-20s-and-30s.html.

Mintzberg, H. (1994). The fall and rise of strategic planning. *Harvard Business Review*. Accessed May 15, 2023, from https://hbr.org/1994/01/the-fall-and-rise-of-strategic-planning.

Moules, J. (2019, January 3). Why MBAs should keep going back to school. *The Financial Times*. Accessed March 12, 2023, from https://www.ft.com/content/257d9aa8-fd69-11e8-ac00-57a2a826423e.

Ohio State University. (2009, October 5). Body posture affects confidence in your own thoughts, study finds. *Science Daily*. Accessed April 23, 2023, from https://www.sciencedaily.com/releases/2009/10/091005111627.htm

Perez, T. (2019, June 4). Earnings peak at different ages for different demographic groups. *Payscale*. Accessed May 15, 2023, from https://www.payscale.com/research-and-insights/peak-earnings/.

Ries, E. (2011). *The lean startup: How today's entrepreneurs use continuous innovation to create radically successful businesses*. Crown Business.

Russell, B. (n.d.). Bertrand Russell quotes. *Goodreads*. Accessed April 23, 2023, from https://www.goodreads.com/quotes/367-do-not-fear-to-be-eccentric-in-opinion-for-every.

Von Bismarck, O. (n.d.). Otto von Bismarck quotes. *Goodreads*. Accessed April 23, 2023, from https://www.goodreads.com/quotes/294225-only-a-fool-learns-from-his-own-mistakes-the-wise.

9

How to Get Value from Your MBA Alumni Network

Lifelong Linkages

Selecting an MBA program is more like a marriage than a date: you bind yourself for a long time—possibly your whole life—and not just for the duration of the program. This is because good business schools offer their alumni numerous benefits, ranging from access to exclusive clubs, and co-branded credit cards to signal "subtly" that you are a graduate of a prestigious school, to privileged offers for the school's executive education programs. Of course, you might also be tempted to try what other business schools have to offer. Staying with the marriage metaphor, not all marriages last a lifetime and not all marriages are always faithful.

Thus, before you say "yes" to an MBA program, think about the time after graduation. Just bear in mind the popular advice of German parents: "Drum prüfe wer sich ewig bindet, ob sich nicht was Besseres findet" (Therefore check who binds himself forever, if something better is not found).[1] There is also the English proverb: "marry in haste, repent at leisure." Having completed an MBA from a particular business school "brands" you for the rest of your life, and the alumni services you can

---

[1] The original "Drum prüfe, wer sich ewig bindet. Ob sich das Herz zum Herzen findet. Der Wahn ist kurz, die Reu ist lang…" is based on Friedrich von Schiller's 1880 famous Poem "Die Glocke."

expect from schools differ widely. Deciding on an MBA program, therefore, requires taking account of long-term benefits; just as you may look for different qualities in a date versus a marriage.

Sadly, only a minority of applicants appear to appreciate the importance of alumni networks when selecting an MBA program. In a worldwide survey of business school applicants, CarringtonCrisp, an education consultancy based in London, found that only 20% of prospective students thought alumni information was important enough to put on a business school's website.[2] We hope that we can convince you to the contrary, and you will take an interest in the quality of alumni networks when selecting a business school. Providing this holds, the obvious question then is what characterizes a good alumni network? Arguably, two important characteristics are the international reach and size of the alumni network. With an annual cohort of over 1000 graduating MBAs, 37% of whom are international,[3] Harvard Business School fares well on both criteria. It boasts an estimated network of 80,000 alumni spread around the globe. INSEAD, with campus locations in Europe, Asia, the Middle East, and North America, also has more than 1000 MBA graduates per year. Again, this translates into a vast alumni network. Other large alumni networks include the Wharton School of the University of Pennsylvania, the Kellogg School of Management at Northwestern University, and Columbia Business School.[4]

University Alumni Networks

Many business schools embedded in a wider university use the university's alumni platform to keep in touch with their MBA graduates. If this is the case, you need to take a close look at the alumni offers of the university and not only at the alumni club of the business school. The Alliance Manchester Business School, for example, is part of the University of Manchester, which prides itself on having the largest alumni

---

[2] The Economist (2017).
[3] Cook (2021).
[4] Lake (2021).

community of any campus-based university in the UK, with more than 500,000 graduates in more than 190 countries around the world. Local alumni coordinators of the University of Manchester operate in over 50 countries, and sometimes the university is represented with multiple hubs in different cities or regions.

Harvard Business School is also part of Harvard University, which counts more than 400,000 alumni from the undergraduate Harvard College and a dozen Graduate and Professional Schools. At the university level, there are nearly 200 Harvard clubs in more than 70 countries. In addition, there is a wide variety of Special Interest Groups (SIGs), ranging from Harvard Alumni for Agriculture and Harvard Alumni in Healthcare to the Harvard Alumni Disaster Preparedness and Response Team and the Harvard Alumni Peking and Chinese Opera Group.[5]

Alumni Network Rankings

Given there is hardly anything in academia that is not ranked these days, there are also alumni network rankings. The Bloomberg BusinessWeek alumni ranking is part of a large annual students, alumni, and recruiters survey that provides the basis for the publication's overall business school ranking. Asking whether "my school's alumni network has helped me build my career," Bloomberg BusinessWeek places Stanford, Harvard, and Dartmouth (Tuck) on top, though it includes only US business schools in its ranking.[6] In contrast, the alumni network ranking by FindMBA, a website owned and operated by a Germany-based company, also includes some non-US schools. In line with the BusinessWeek ranking, FindMBA lists Stanford, Harvard, and Dartmouth as the top three "most powerful" alumni Networks, but then puts Henley Business School, INSEAD, and HEC Paris in ranks 4–6, respectively.[7] However, the basis for the ranking published by FindMBA is shrouded in mystery. In an article titled "Who you know, not what you know," The Economist

---

[5] Harvard Alumni (n.d.).
[6] Bloomberg (n.d.).
[7] FIND MBA (n.d.).

finally identifies 15 business schools with the highest-ranked alumni networks.[8] Although the article mentions some benefits of alumni networks, such as discounts for executive courses, publications, and financial services, it does not comment on the exact basis for the ranking.

Rank	Business School	Country
1	Henley Business School	United Kingdom
2	HEC School of Management Paris	France
3	INSEAD	France
4	University of Warwick—Warwick Business School	United Kingdom
5	University of California at Berkeley—Haas School of Business	United States
6	Northwestern University—Kellogg School of Management	United States
7	New York University—Leonard N Stern School of Business	United States
8	Indiana University—Kelley School of Business	United States
9	University of Notre Dame—Mendoza College of Business	United States
10	University of Navarra—IESE Business School	Spain
11	Harvard Business School	United States
12	University of Southern California—Marshall School of Business	United States
13	London Business School	United Kingdom
14	IMD—International Institute for Management Development	Switzerland
15	University of Chicago—Booth School of Business	United States

While size is an important criterion driving the range of services alumni networks offer, some MBA admissions consultants emphasize the strengths of smaller networks.[9] They argue that the personal links that can be forged in smaller alumni associations are of higher quality.

---

[8] The Economist (2017).
[9] Lake (2021).

Friends with Benefits

To decide which aspects of an alumni association are most useful in your individual circumstances, we recommend taking a closer look at the benefits you can expect from a good school's alumni network. Of course, we again group the benefits under eight headings: lucky number—by now you know the routine.

1. Access to the Business School's Alumni Networking

The financial barriers to becoming a member of an alumni network are low. After graduation, and in some cases already a few months prior to graduation, an alumni association typically charges a modest fee of €20–€100 per year and offers the option of a lifetime membership. In fact, some alumni networks are entirely free of charge.[10] But why get involved? First and foremost, you may gain access to influential members of the alumni association. Celebrity CEOs like Elon Musk or Warren Buffett belong to the alumni network of Wharton Business School and Columbia Business School, respectively. Yet, even though high-flying celebrity executives who graduated from the same business school will give you some bragging opportunities, you may still be unable to reach out to them for a one-on-one chat. On the other hand, you may be able to establish links with some senior managers in an industry or country you are particularly interested in. In fact, some lesser-known individuals in an industry that are of relevance to you could actually be very helpful to you.

Another important aspect of access to the network is the frequency and quality of meetings and events the alumni association organizes. If the only activity of the network is one annual "homecoming" meeting somewhere in Texas, and you happen to be based in Singapore, the network may not be as useful to you as a network with a chapter in Singapore that meets on a monthly basis. That said, it is not only the frequency of the personal meetings you should scrutinize. Important is also the existence and usage of social networks on online platforms. These days, most alumni associations run such networks, such as closed groups on LinkedIn, but the frequency and quality of participation in these

---

[10] Carlton (2022).

networks vary considerably. Most LinkedIn groups function as merely member directories rather than as discussion platforms. So, keep your expectations low on how active these groups are and instead use them to gauge who the members are and how senior they are. And if you need to discuss something with fellow alumni, it is best to approach individuals directly or via the introduction of a mutual friend/contact.

2. Access to Career Services

For many MBA graduates, the degree is a vehicle to launch into a new job. For Executive MBAs who are already in a job, an MBA degree often offers an opportunity to reflect on their current position, on new horizons, and on the possibilities for career change or career acceleration. Thus, alumni career services are not only of use to newly-minted MBAs who look for a first job after graduation, but are equally relevant to seasoned executives who might already be quite advanced in their careers.

Notwithstanding the potential usefulness of career services for experienced executives, alumni organizations typically also open their services to MBA students prior to graduation. London Business School (LBS), for example, offers a "Job Board" and "CV Database," that can be searched by employers. Notably, the LBS alumni network has a reciprocal arrangement with job boards from a select set of partner schools, namely Harvard Business School, Kellogg, INSEAD, Stanford and Columbia. Even in the era of LinkedIn, this makes searching rather attractive for top employers and offers MBA graduates a wider reach.[11] Leading European business schools, INSEAD, HEC-Paris, IESE, LBS, and Rotterdam School of Management, also organize jointly (in two slightly different formations) an Asia Career Fair and a LatAm Career Fair.

Bocconi, like many other leading business schools, offers career coaching as part of its alumni services, while WU-Vienna offers executive coaching to its EMBA students as part of the program. Again, this not only supports graduates searching for a first job after their MBA, but is also geared to executives, who wish to engage with professional coaches to reflect on career progress, explore plans to change jobs, or prepare for

---

[11] London Business School (n.d.).

the next promotion. Bocconi complements its career coaching with training seminars and workshops on personal and professional development as well as online self-assessment tools.[12]

Closely related to professional coaching is mentoring. For example, the Cox School of Business at the Southern Methodist University (Dallas, Texas) offers two types of mentoring. One approach, the so-called flash mentoring, provides MBA students with an opportunity to have an in-depth conversation with a business leader who is a Cox alum. In the other approach, the school teams up MBA students with alumni for a whole year. During this time, students can regularly turn to their mentors for career advice.[13]

3. Access to Selected Course Offerings

Learning does not finish with graduation. In an increasingly turbulent environment, where technological changes have the ability to destroy and create entire industries, it is a must to engage in lifelong learning. Good alumni associations support lifelong learning in numerous ways. Some offer alumni a limited number of seats in their regular MBA classrooms; others open their e-learning platforms and discussion forums to alumni or offer access to teaching materials uploaded by professors. Alumni conferences focusing on specific topics or subgroups centering on specific industries also encourage lifelong learning.

Nearly all business schools offer their alumni discounts for their executive education portfolio. During the past few years, the nature of these courses has been changing. Broad comprehensive month-long programs are increasingly replaced by short "top-up" skill-development courses where participants can gain certificates. Approximately 40% of AACSB-accredited business schools offer graduate-level certificates.[14] In the future, these stackable certificates have the potential to upend the entire

---

[12] Bocconi Alumni (n.d.-b).
[13] Kelly (2021).
[14] Thomas (2020).

business model of business schools,[15] replacing the one-time MBA degree with a lifelong subscription model.

4. Access to Webinars

Webinars, also referred to as webcasts, are part of a lifelong learning portfolio that every MBA graduate should utilize. They are less time-consuming than attending courses in person or following online programs. Webinars tend to be relatively short and do not require any active participation or coursework from participants. Members of good alumni networks usually have free access to a wide variety of webinar topics, which are either offered by the alumni organization itself or by the respective business school or university. Wharton alumni, for example, get access to a webcast library that includes the following topics:

- Analytics
- COVID-19
- Economics & Public Policy
- Entrepreneurship
- Finance
- Healthcare
- International
- Law & Ethics
- Leadership
- Management
- Marketing
- Operations, Information & Decisions
- Personal & Professional Development
- Technology

Under each heading, alumni can find a list of about a dozen hour-long webinars, often hosted by Wharton professors. If speakers make their slide sets available, the webcasts provide download links. Of course, alumni can also attend webinars synchronously, i.e., as a live transmission;

---

[15] Schlegelmilch (2020).

or asynchronously, i.e., as a pre-recorded transmission. Live webcasts have the obvious advantage that the information is more up-to-date. More importantly, live webcasts permit alumni to submit questions through a chat function, which the speaker will address as time permits.

Taken collectively, high-quality webcasts are a hallmark of good alumni associations and offer real ongoing benefits to their members, be it to keep up-to-date on a range of topics or to obtain career advice and learn about topics such as building your personal brand, your portfolio career, durable relationships, and much more.[16]

5. Access to Bespoke Events

Some alumni associations are able to offer their members exclusive events to interact with politicians or corporate leaders, who are usually difficult to access. Examples range from an evening with the Ambassador of the Sultanate of Oman arranged by the Harvard Club of Washington[17]; to a dinner with the Managing Director of Campari Germany hosted by Bocconi[18]; to a talk and cocktail reception with the CEO of Xerox, organized by IESE Alumni.[19] Clearly, alumni associations of business schools with strong brand names and/or an advantageous location in a global city have more opportunities to attract top speakers to their events.

However, bespoke events do not only refer to events with prominent speakers. Some alumni clubs are also able to offer their members access to interesting buildings or places. This may include a backstage tour of a famous opera house, a visit to a palace that is usually closed to the public, or an exclusive wine-tasting event at a famous winery. Once again, the quality of events alumni associations offer varies considerably and is indicative of the value they represent.

---

[16] INSEAD (n.d.).
[17] Harvard Club of Washington, DC (n.d.).
[18] Bocconi Alumni (n.d.-a).
[19] IESE Alumni (n.d.).

6. Subscription to Business Schools' Newsletters

A good alumni magazine or newsletter can offer additional benefits. First, graduates typically receive selected articles on professional development, leadership, and various topical issues as well as information about the research activities of the business school's faculty. Second, the magazine or newsletter reports on important events at the business school and the university at large, and alerts alumni of relevant forthcoming meetings. Third, the alumni magazine creates a bond and a sense of family[20] among graduates by sharing professional and private news (e.g., new role appointments, job promotions, and weddings) of fellow alumni.

According to the Council for Advancement and Support of Education (CASE), the vast majority of alumni magazines are online and most are distributed no more than two or three times per year.[21] However, some magazines also combine print with podcasts.[22] While most business schools limit the circulation of their alumni magazines to alumni, there are some noteworthy exceptions. The very impressive alumni magazine of Columbia University, for example, can be freely downloaded by anyone.[23] In addition, Columbia Business School provides an online resource with feature articles, podcasts, videos, and webinars, as well as a magazine, research, and press section. The school clearly recognizes the strategic importance of alumni to student recruitment and image building.

MBA alumni from AMBA-accredited business schools also have access to the AMBA magazine "AMBITION," which targets the MBA community in general. AMBA publishes ten issues of the magazine each year. The online version is free of charge, while the printed version requires a modest subscription fee. The content is tailored to MBA graduates and includes challenging articles, interviews with industry and business school leaders, best practice case studies, and practical takeaways.[24]

---

[20] Kester (2008).
[21] CASE (n.d.).
[22] Oleisky (2018).
[23] Columbia Magazine (n.d.).
[24] AMBA (n.d.).

7. Access to Alumni Sports Clubs and Recreational Events

A number of business schools and universities organize events ranging from golf tournaments, to running events (marathons, 5K or 10K) to water polo alumni weekends. Typically, sports clubs associated with a business school or university are not exclusive to alumni but also include current students. To this end, these clubs and events are not only good for your health, but offer platforms to keep in touch with your alma mater and to keep abreast of current developments through contact with students.

8. Access to Unusual Alumni Benefits and Bragging Opportunities

Alumni of the University of California at Berkeley can rent an entire mountain retreat located in the Sierra Nevada for corporate gatherings, family reunions, or weddings—apparently even when your partner does not hold a University of California degree. Oxford and Cambridge graduates can get admitted to an exclusive London-based members club creatively named "Oxford and Cambridge Club" (subject to endorsement by two current members). Washington State University hosts an alumni wine club, while a Harvard degree opens the route to a Harvard Alumni World MasterCard®. And just in case a MasterCard® is too inconspicuous, graduates from the Thunderbird School of Global Management can acquire a Thunderbird-branded license plate for their car, albeit only legally possible if the car is registered in Arizona. To help alumni show off their association to their business school, an investment in a university ring may help. The tradition to purchase a "graduating class" ring dates back to the United States Military Academy at West Point in 1835 and, until today, it is mainly popular in the United States. That said, university rings will get you noticed "even across crowded airport terminals the world over" (as one business school, which should remain anonymous to be saved from embarrassment, claims on its alumni website). If a co-branded credit card, a license plate for your car, and a university ring are still too subtle, you can draw more attention by wearing an appropriately branded university baseball cap, T-shirt, sweat pants or buy some children's apparel for your offspring. Hardly any branding opportunity remains untouched by marketing-savvy alumni managers.

Summary

Many potential MBA applicants appear to neglect the importance of a business school's alumni network when deciding where to apply. We argue that this is short-sighted. The school that awards your MBA brands you for life, and the benefits you can draw from your degree are influenced by the quality of the alumni network and its activities. Although in the times of social media, contacts can be managed via LinkedIn and Facebook,[25] and get-togethers can be organized via Meetup or InterNations, alumni associations continue to provide unique benefits for their members. Support of fellow alumni when searching for a new job or changing an old one, access to lifelong career services, bespoke learning opportunities, as well as opportunities for students and alumni to interact, are difficult to replicate by social media platforms. However, above all, it is the sense of belonging and grounding in an increasingly busy and transactional business environment that makes alumni associations truly valuable.

References

AMBA. (n.d.) *Education & business magazine.* Accessed October 28, 2022, from https://www.associationofmbas.com/ambition.

Bloomberg. (n.d.) The best business schools as scored by alumni. *Bloomberg.* Accessed October 24, 2022, from https://www.bloomberg.com/business-schools/2018/insights/alumni-scores/?leadSource=uverify%20wall#xj4y7vzkg.

Bocconi Alumni. (n.d.-a). *A conversation with Andrea Neri.* Accessed October 27, 2022, from https://www.bocconialumni.it/permalink/content/a-conversation-with-andrea-neri.

Bocconi Alumni. (n.d.-b). *Career advice.* Accessed October 25, 2022, from https://www.bocconialumni.it/career-advice.

Carlton, G. (2022). Ten benefits of joining an alumni association. *TheBestSchools.* Accessed October 25, 2022, from https://thebestschools.org/magazine/benefits-joining-alumni-association/#:~:text=Alumni%20associations%20

---

[25] CUSEUM (2021).

typically%20cost%20%2420-%24100%20per%20year%20or,and%20 alumni%20associations%20aren%27t%20just%20for%20recent%20 graduates.

CASE. (n.d.) *Alumni magazines: By the numbers.* Accessed October 28, 2022, from https://www.case.org/resources/alumni-magazines-numbers.

Columbia Magazine. (n.d.) *Homepage.* Accessed October 28, 2022, from https://magazine.columbia.edu.

Cook, S. (2021, November 3). Harvard MBA class profile | Breakdown. *BusinessBecause.* Accessed October 24, 2022, from https://www.businessbecause.com/news/mba-class-profile/7419/harvard-mba-class-profile.

CUSEUM. (2021, July 8). 5 tips to offer valuable alumni benefits in the twenty-first century. *CUSEUM.* Accessed October 30, 2022, from https://cuseum.com/blog/2021/7/8/5-tips-to-offer-valuable-alumni-benefits-in-the-twenty-first-century.

FIND MBA. (n.d.) Top 10 MBA programs with the most powerful alumni networks. *FIND MBA.* Accessed October 24, 2022, from https://find-mba.com/lists/top-10-mba-programs-with-the-most-powerful-alumni-networks.

Harvard Alumni. (n.d.) *Welcome to the Harvard Alumni Association.* Accessed October 24, 2022, from https://alumni.harvard.edu/community.

Harvard Club of Washington, DC. (n.d.) *Sold out: In person: An evening with the ambassador of the Sultanate of Oman, HE Moosa Hamdan Al Tai.* Accessed October 27, 2022, from https://hcdc.clubs.harvard.edu/article.html?aid=2364.

IESE Alumni. (n.d.) *Digital transformation: A conversation with Steve Bandrowczak, CEO at Xerox.* Accessed October 27, 2022, from https://alumni.iese.edu/events/94934.

INSEAD. (n.d.) *Career development.* Accessed October 26, 2022, from https://www.insead.edu/alumni/career-development.

Kelly, M. (2021, January 31). What to look for in an MBA alumni network. *Noodle.* Accessed October 25, 2022, from https://resources.noodle.com/articles/what-to-look-for-in-an-mba-alumni-network/.

Kester, E. (2008, December 1). Alumni: A sense of family in an increasing commercial world. *The Financial Times.* Accessed October 28, 2022, from https://www.ft.com/content/f7d92238-bce2-11dd-af5a-0000779fd18c.

Lake, S. (2021, July 16). The best MBA alumni networks. *Fortune.* Accessed October 24, 2022, from https://fortune.com/education/articles/the-best-mba-alumni-networks/.

London Business School. (n.d.) *Alumni*. Accessed October 25, 2022, from https://www.london.edu/alumni.

Oleisky, J. (2018, August 21). The staying power of alumni magazines. *Kalixmarketing*. Accessed October 28, 2022, from https://kalixmarketing.com/staying-power-alumni-magazines/.

Schlegelmilch, B. B. (2020). Why business schools need radical innovations: Drivers and development trajectories. *Journal of Marketing Education, 42*(2), 93–107.

The Economist. (2017, March 24). Who you know, not what you know. *The Economist*. Accessed October 24, 2022, from https://www.economist.com/whichmba/mba-rankings/alumni-network.

Thomas, P. (2020, Nov. 13; R6). The future of everything: The education issue - The constant M.B.A.: Elite business schools offer lifelong learning. *Wall Street Journal*, Eastern Edition, New York.

von Schiller, F. (1880). Das Lied von der Glocke. *teachSam*. Accessed May 17, 2023, from http://teachsam.de/deutsch/d_literatur/d_aut/sci/sci_lyr/sci_lyr_bal/sci_ball_txt_1.htm.

10

Why You Should Already Think About the Long-term Impact of Your MBA Degree

Thinking About the Future Informs Your Choices

Albert Einstein famously declared, "I never think of the future—it comes soon enough."[1] With advancing age, one tends to become increasing sympathetic about his sentiment. However, we contend that as a prospective MBA student, you are well advised to think about the impact you would like to make in the long term. While the future is difficult to predict, an idea about the field in which you would like to make an impact will inform your choice of business school and the choice of electives.

Strive for an Ikigai Future

Another argument for thinking about your long-term impact goes back to the Ikigai concept introduced in the first chapter of this book. Arguably, you are not only in this world to maximize your income. Instead, you maximize your joy and happiness when you devote your energy to a field at the intersection between what you love to do, what you are good at,

---

[1] Einstein (1930).

what the world needs, and what you can be paid for. But how does one find this magic field that holds the key reason for being? As we know from the Kama Sutra, there is more than one way to happiness. We focus once again on eight broad fields (lucky number), where you may want to make a contribution. Our approach coincides with the PESTELED framework, which is frequently used in international business to guide and structure the analysis of foreign market environments.[2] The acronym stands for **P**olitical, **E**conomic, **S**ocial, **T**echnological, **E**nvironmental, **L**egal, **E**thical, and **D**emographics factors.

1. Political: Improving Government and Public Affairs

A good part of any MBA course tends to be devoted to leadership. This relates to the development of competences, skills, and characteristics that help to align people around a common goal or purpose. Thus, at the end of a successful MBA program, you should have a sufficient grounding to put leadership into practice. This does not necessarily have to be in a corporate environment but can also be in politics. In fact, an MBA degree and a subsequent career in politics appear to gel well.[3] Among the most prominent examples are the British Prime Minister Rishi Sunak (Stanford Graduate School of Business), the former US president George W. Bush (Harvard Business School), and, last but not least, the Prime Minister of Tonga, Siaosi 'Ofakivahafolau Sovaleni (University of the South Pacific). While one explanation of the increasing prominence of MBAs in politics is the need for greater professionalism in government, unsurprisingly for politics, the opinion is divided about the effectiveness of MBA politicians.[4] Still, if a leadership position in politics appeals to you, you may want to look at business schools that have a leaning towards the public sector or government. At the George Washington School of Business, some 12% of MBA graduates went into government roles.[5] A number of business schools, notably Oxford's Saïd Business School and Johns Hopkins University Carey Business School also offer options to their

---

[2] Schlegelmilch (2022).
[3] Schiller (2011).
[4] Lister (2019).
[5] FIND MBA (n.d.-d).

MBAs to pursue dual degrees with a Master of Public Policy (MPP) or a Master of Arts in Government (MA). Other business schools have relevant MBA concentrations, such as York University's Schulich School of Business, where students can focus on the "Public Sector," or the Business School of the University of Alberta, where a specialization in "Public Policy & Management" is on offer. Furthermore, some of the top US business schools may "forgive" your tuition loan altogether if you take up a government job after graduation and work in government for a number of years. In sum, an MBA may set you up nicely for a career in a government department or in politics.

2. Economic: Working in Industry and Commerce
Insights provided by economics are predominantly theoretical, and largely aimed at providing a big-picture perspective. Although MBA students typically demand a more practice-based orientation from their professors, there is nothing more useful to practicing managers than a guiding framework and a sound theory. If you are among those (future) managers who are interested in a deeper theoretical understanding, you may want to seek out economics-oriented MBA programs. While such programs enhance your understanding of the influence of economic principles on business and sharpen your quantitative skills, you need to bear in mind that an MBA is an interdisciplinary degree that focuses on a wide variety of subjects useful for *business administration*. Thus, the depth of economic teaching in the context of an MBA program is less than in a degree that focuses exclusively on economics, such as an MSc in economics. Even MBAs in Economics will typically offer economics as a specialization or concentration that follows a larger set of mandatory core courses.[6] The specialization, for example, may include courses in macroeconomics, microeconomics, mathematics, and statistics for economics or econometrics. Business schools that offer a specialization in economics include New York University's Stern School of Business,[7] the University of

---

[6] MBA Central (n.d.).
[7] NYU Stern (n.d.).

Minnesota's Carlson School,[8] the University of Chicago,[9] and IE Business School in Madrid,[10] to name but a few.[11] A sound understanding of economics is essential early on in your career. Just think of the significance of establishing a breakeven point or the price elasticity of demand concept. A solid understanding of economics will also help you at a later stage in your career when your role is more likely to have a global remit: from informing your strategy on foreign currency transactions and investment flows to signing global trade deals. While business schools have different economics specializations in their MBA programs, all are aimed at encouraging big-picture thinking that will help you in your role as a future manager.

3. Social: Striving for Social Impact

One does not have to look far to find social challenges and problems. They may be broad topics such as hunger, poverty, and healthcare provisions, or specific issues such as mandatory vaccinations, LGBT+ adoption rights, and online privacy concerns. Regardless, social problems are often passionately debated, as they tend to be sources of conflicting opinions. At the same time, social issues are also complex and overlap with other aspects. Healthcare provision, for example, has economic, legal, and ethical implications and provides technological challenges. Thus, if you do not shy away from complex problems and feel passionate about social issues, an MBA with a focus on social issues might be the right choice for you.[12] Although an MBA may not sound like an obvious pathway for a career devoted to solving social issues, businesses put a growing focus on their corporate social responsibility (CSR) and try to address social issues while making a profit. You could also join or found a benefit corporation (B Corp) that, alongside profits, explicitly commits to pursuing socially responsible standards. Finally, there are countless Non-profit

---

[8] University of Minnesota (n.d.).
[9] Chicago Booth (n.d.).
[10] FIND MBA (n.d.-a).
[11] For additional business schools offering specializations in economics, see also Master's Programs Guide (2023) and FIND MBA (n.d.-b).
[12] Meley (2022).

Organizations that seek managerial insights. Thus, an MBA could be a better launch to a socially oriented career than you may have thought.

4. Technological: Enabling the Future
Nothing is more significant in transforming our society than technology, and right now, we are in the midst of turbulent digital transformation processes that affect nearly all aspects of our lives. Thus, if you see yourself working with new technology, you will be closer to the future than in virtually any other area.

Technology affine MBAs might be attracted to typical IT careers, such as Chief Technology Officer, IT Director, or Chief Information Officer. Some MBAs have made it right to the C-Suite. The CEO of Google, Sundar Pichai, graduated with an MBA from the Wharton School of the University of Pennsylvania,[13] Amazon CEO Andy Jassy received his MBA from Harvard Business School,[14] Microsoft CEO Satya Nadella received his MBA from the Booth School of Business at the University of Chicago,[15] and Apple's Tim Cook earned his MBA at the Fuqua School of Duke University.[16] Last, MBAs in Technology Management are also eminently suitable to become entrepreneurs themselves. Given the central role technology plays in many newly founded companies, the combination of technical knowledge and management know-how will be a valuable asset.

Among the business schools that should be considered by prospective MBA students with an affinity for technology are, for example, the University of Washington's Foster School of Business in Seattle which placed 45% of its 2022 MBA graduates in technology companies.[17] MIT Sloan School of Management in Boston, which even has technology in its name, placed 23% of its most recent cohort in technology,[18] and the University of California Los Angeles, UCLA Anderson School of

---

[13] Rosenberg (2022).
[14] Kefford (2021).
[15] Microsoft (n.d.).
[16] Apple (n.d.).
[17] Foster School of Business (n.d.).
[18] MIT SLOAN (2022).

Management with a technology placement rate of 33%.[19] In Europe, you may wish to explore the Technical University of Munich (TUM), which offers an Executive MBA in Business & IT,[20] or the Judge Business School of the University of Cambridge, which has an excellent reputation for E-commerce and Internet technology and runs a concentration in Digital Transformation.[21] However, there are also many other excellent technology-based MBA offers, and not only in the USA or Europe.

5. Environmental: Protecting our Environment

There is general agreement that the world needs to take urgent actions to save our environment. The well-known slogan "There is no Planet B" powerfully demonstrates this sentiment. Unfortunately, there is less agreement on the specifics, such as who should do what by when. As business ultimately depends on a healthy environment, progressive business schools increasingly develop MBA programs that focus on different environmental topics. Such programs are offered by rather diverse institutions, such as an Energy Management MBA offered by the TU of Berlin, Germany,[22] an MBA in Sustainable Innovation by the Gustavson School of Business, University of Victoria, Canada,[23] or an MBA with a Specialization in Sustainability at the University of Haifa, Israel. Audencia Business School in Nantes (France) has a reputation for sustainability in Europe. Rankings of Business Schools focusing on Energy and Natural Resources are also available.[24]

MBA specializations in sustainability management or environmental management are typically interdisciplinary specializations that draw on social science, environmental science, and advanced technology knowledge. The job prospects in the field tend to be strong, as companies and regulatory bodies pay increasing attention to environmental factors. In fact, research shows that companies with high environmental, social, and

---

[19] UCLA Anderson School of Management (n.d.).
[20] TUM (n.d.).
[21] University of Cambridge (n.d.).
[22] TU Berlin (n.d.).
[23] University of Victoria (n.d.).
[24] FIND MBA (n.d.-c).

governance standards outperform the market,[25] indicating that these types of jobs are likely to be future-proof. Industry positions for MBAs who have specialized in environmental management or sustainability carry titles such as Sustainability Officer, Head of Sustainability, Principle Ecologist, Renewable Energy Director, or Environmental Project Officer. Consulting companies, NGOs, the UN, or different government departments also employ suitably-trained MBAs. Thus, if you would like to devote your career to creating a more sustainable future, an MBA program specializing in environmental management or sustainability may just be right for you.

6. Legal: Managing the Interface of Law and Business
Pursuing an MBA degree is time-consuming and requires considerable effort and commitment. Consequently, top MBA programs attract some rather ambitious people. Among those, there is a small segment whose ambition and dedication even surpasses that of the already highly-charged MBA crowd. They pursue two degrees simultaneously: a joint Juris Doctor (JD) and MBA degree. Although these joint/dual degree programs are often truly daunting, they are more time-efficient and usually less costly than pursuing both degrees separately. The reward for the ambitious souls who complete such joint degrees are excellent job prospects and flexibility in designing their careers.

The versatility of jobs for graduates with a JD/MBA degree is evidenced by scanning relevant websites, where the degree is seen as a possible foundation for such diverse careers as Corporate Lawyer, Director of Finance, or even working for the Federal Bureau of Investigation (FBI), presumably only open to US citizens.[26,27] Various rankings of business schools offering joint JD/MBA degrees in the US are available.[28,29] However, there are also reputable business schools that offer combined

---

[25] Bonini and Swartz (2014).
[26] Dolan (2021).
[27] Indeed (2021).
[28] College Gegazette (2021).
[29] Scott (2021).

law and MBA degrees in Europe (e.g., IE in Madrid),[30] Asia, for example the Chinese University of Hong Kong (CUHK),[31] Australia, for instance, the University of New South Wales in Sydney[32] and elsewhere.

7. Ethical: Supporting Moral Principles

While business ethics, corporate social responsibility (CSR), and sustainability focus on slightly different domains, together they are trying to make the world a better place and represent a "force for good."[33] This makes working in these fields psychologically rewarding. However, the emphasis is on psychological! Financially, jobs such as CSR Director, Community Affairs Manager, Ethics Officer, Ethics & Compliance Director, or Social Impact and Sustainability Director are usually not at the top of the corporate earnings ladder. Yet, clearly, money is not everything, and the job satisfaction one can derive may weigh more than the pecuniary remuneration.

While there is a substantial overlap between CSR and sustainability,[34] CSR and business ethics jobs primarily focus on people, whereas positions in sustainability (see point 5 on Environment) primarily focus on our ecological environment. A key characteristic of CSR is that companies go beyond their minimum legal requirements and obligations in order to address societal needs.[35] Accordingly, most CSR and ethics-related corporate jobs go beyond compliance. Some have an external focus, designing impactful community outreach programs, corporate philanthropy, and sponsoring activities. Others focus inwards, ensuring a safe and fair work environment for employees. If you aspire to pursue a career in any of these areas, you can find MBA programs that build their entire curriculum around CSR issues.[36,37] Alternatively, many MBA

---

[30] IE University (n.d.).
[31] CUHK (n.d.).
[32] UNSW Sydney (n.d.-a).
[33] Schlegelmilch and Szőcs (2020).
[34] Sheehy and Farneti (2021).
[35] Lopes-Rodriguez and Smith (2021).
[36] Questrom School of Business (n.d.).
[37] The Heller School at Brandeis University (n.d.).

programs, such as INSEAD,[38] Hong Kong University Business School,[39] or the Business School of the University of New South Wales in Sydney[40] offer appropriate specialization options.

8. Demographics: Analyzing Challenges Relating to Population Development

The French philosopher Auguste Comte stated: "demography is destiny."[41] While this is arguably an overstatement, demography is of central importance for many countries, and ultimately for the world as a whole. Recently, the Japanese Prime Minister Fumio Kishida warned: "Our nation is on the cusp of whether it can maintain its societal functions."[42] The reason for his concern is clear: by 2060, the Japanese population is predicted to decline from the current 128 million to 87 million people, 40% of whom will be retired.[43] A shrinking workforce between 15 and 65, an aging population, a "hostility to immigration," and an increasing number of Japanese below 30, who are not living in a relationship and are uninterested in producing babies,[44] make for an explosive mix of social problems. While shrinking populations and aging are of concern for some countries, others are worried about dramatic population increases. Until 2050, more than half of the world's population growth is predicted to occur in only nine countries, topped by India, Nigeria, and Pakistan. As of 2023, India is the world's most populous country, replacing China which is facing a shrinking population.[45] Nigeria is predicted to outrank the US as the third most populous country by 2050. [46] As we elaborated elsewhere, whether the world is suffering more from population growth or from population shortage very much depends on an individual's

---

[38] INSEAD (n.d.).
[39] HKU Business School (n.d.).
[40] UNSW Sydney (n.d.-b).
[41] Comte (n.d.).
[42] Bhardwaj (2023).
[43] BBC (2012).
[44] Wingfield-Hayes (2023).
[45] The Economist (2023).
[46] Sasu (2022).

country perspective. The demographic trends are clear, but their implications are muddy and paradoxical.[47]

If you are intrigued by the causes and consequences of population changes, such as migration and immigration, aging, or population control, and you are aspiring a job related to demographics, an MBA is admittedly not the most direct route, although occasionally, some MBA programs offer electives that discuss demography under the heading "business and big problems."[48] That said, if you have a leaning towards statistics, economics, or quantitative social science, there are possibilities in government departments of organizations like the UN. In commercial companies, it is the Business Development Analysts, Policy Analysts, or Strategic Information and Evaluation Specialists who attempt to predict how demographic changes impact on future business opportunities. Here an MBA will be a useful background.

Summary

Thinking about the future is difficult, and predicting the future is often no more than guesswork. We still think it is a useful exercise that can guide you to find an MBA program that is right for you. Thinking about the kind of jobs likely to be needed in future, reflecting on what you enjoy doing, what you are good at, and how important money is likely to be for you in leading a balanced and happy life will steer you to MBA programs and specializations that become enablers for the professional life you like to lead in future.

In this chapter, we presented our thoughts on eight broad fields in which you may want to make a contribution. Of course, we readily admit that there are more possibilities. However, in keeping with the spirit of this book—*a guide to success* that follows a pattern of *eight steps*—we stuck to the "lucky eight." We hope this brings you luck—the mysterious ingredient that may crown all your efforts and hard work. Ultimately, we hope that our guidance will not only help you *find an MBA program that fits*

---

[47] Schlegelmilch (2022).
[48] Harvard Business School (2023).

your needs but will also contribute a little to finding your very personal Ikigai.

However, we would also like to leave you with a story about how changing the world trumps changing yourself: Two famous American intellectuals, Noam Chomsky and Gore Vidal, clashed in 1991 in their only joint TV interview ever recorded. They were asked what was their driving force and source of motivation. Noam Chomsky gave a good answer: "Looking in the mirror in the morning and not being appalled at what I see." However, Gore Vidal's response was even better: "For me, it's looking out the window and not being appalled at what I see."[49]

Indeed, there is a world to change out there. So go do it, one MBA at a time!

References

Apple. (n.d.) *Tim Cook*. Accessed January 7, 2023, from https://www.apple.com/leadership/tim-cook/.

BBC. (2012, January 30). Japan population to shrink by one-third by 2060. *BBC News*. Accessed January 26, 2023, from https://www.bbc.com/news/world-asia-16787538.

Bhardwaj, M. (2023, January 25). Japan PM vows against declining population. *Asiana Times*. Accessed January 26, 2023, from https://asianatimes.com/japanese-pm-vows-against-declining-population/.

Bonini, S. & Swartz, S. (2014). Profits with purpose: How organizing for sustainability can benefit the bottom line. *McKinsey & Company*. Accessed January 22, 2023, from https://www.mckinsey.com/~/media/McKinsey/Business%20Functions/Sustainability/Our%20Insights/Profits%20with%20purpose/Profits%20with%20Purpose.ashx.

Chicago Booth. (n.d.) *MBA economics*. Accessed January 5, 2023, from https://www.chicagobooth.edu/mba/academics/curriculum/concentrations/economics.

Chomsky, N. & Vidal, G. (1991). In conversation with Gore Vidal and Noam Chomsky (1991). [Video]. *Youtube*. Accessed April 12, 2023, from https://www.youtube.com/watch?v=k5Iv3btFIW8&ab_channel=megakeenbeen.

---

[49] Chomsky and Vidal (1991).

College Gegazette. (2021, August 25). The 10 best MBA JD programs in the US. *College Gegazette*. Accessed January 24, 2023, from https://collegegazette.com/best-mba-jd-programs-in-the-us/.

Comte, A. (n.d.) Auguste Comte quotes. *Goodreads*. Accessed January 26, 2023, from https://www.goodreads.com/quotes/8746229-demography-is-destiny.

CUHK. (n.d.) *Full-time MBA JD/MBA*. Accessed January 24, 2023, from https://mba.cuhk.edu.hk/programmes/full-time-mba/jd-mba/.

Dolan, C. (2021). What careers are available with a JD/MBA?. *Nonprofit Colleges Online*. Accessed January 23, 2023, from https://www.nonprofitcollegesonline.com/faq/jd-mba-careers/.

Einstein, A. (1930). *I never think of the future. It comes soon enough. Quote Investigator*. Accessed January 1, 2023, from https://quoteinvestigator.com/2013/07/23/future-soon/.

FIND MBA. (n.d.-a). IE business schools. *FIND MBA*. Accessed January 5, 2023, from https://find-mba.com/schools/europe/spain/ie/programs.

FIND MBA. (n.d.-b). MBA programs in economics – Europe. *FIND MBA*. Accessed January 5, 2023, from https://find-mba.com/schools/europe/specialization/economics#:~:text=MBA%20Programs%20in%20Economics%20-%20Europe%201%20IE,-%20Graduate%20School%20of%20International%20Business%20%28GSIB%29%20.

FIND MBA. (n.d.-c). Top business schools for energy and natural resources 2022. *FIND MBA*. Accessed January 24, 2023, from https://find-mba.com/lists/top-business-schools-for-energy-and-natural-resources.

FIND MBA. (n.d.-d). Top business schools for public sector management/government 2022. *FIND MBA*. Accessed January 3, 2023, from https://find-mba.com/lists/top-business-schools-for-public-sector-management-government.

Foster School of Business. (n.d.) *Full-time MBA career management*. Accessed January 7, 2023, from https://foster.uw.edu/academics/degree-programs/full-time-mba/career-management/.

Harvard Business School. (2023). *Reimagining capitalism: Business and big problems*. Accessed January 26, 2023, from https://www.hbs.edu/coursecatalog/1524.html.

HKU Business School. (n.d.) *Full-time MBA*. Accessed January 26, 2023, from https://mba.hkubs.hku.hk/programmes/full-time-mba/academics/curriculum-structure/.

ie University. (n.d.) *Dual Degree International MBA + Master of Laws (LL.M.)*. Accessed January 24, 2023, from https://www.ie.edu/masters/dual-degrees/programs/dual-degree-international-mba-master-of-laws-llm/.

Indeed. (2021, June 8). *15 High-paying jobs you can get with a J.D./MBA degree*. Accessed January 23, 2023, from https://www.indeed.com/career-advice/finding-a-job/jd-mba-jobs.

INSEAD. (n.d.) *New MBA curriculum*. Accessed January 26, 2023, from https://www.insead.edu/master-programmes/mba/academics#curriculum-overview.

Kefford, M. (2021, February 3). Who is Andy Jassy? Amazon CEO & Harvard MBA Graduate. *BusinessBecause*. Accessed January 7, 2023, from https://www.businessbecause.com/news/mba-degree/7456/andy-jassy.

Lister, A. (2019, December 4). 5 Controversial politicians with MBAs. *BusinessBecause*. Accessed January 3, 2023, from https://www.businessbecause.com/news/mba-degree/6355/5-controversial-politicians-mba.

Lopes-Rodriguez, S., & Smith, N. C. (2021). Marketing strategy and corporate social responsibility. In B. B. Schlegelmilch & R. S. Winer (Eds.), *The Routledge companion to strategic marketing*. Routledge.

Master's Programs Guide. (2023). 10 best economics MBA programs. *Mastersprogramsguide*. Accessed January 5, 2023, from https://www.mastersprogramsguide.com/rankings/best-mba-economics/.

MBA Central. (n.d.) What can I do with an economics MBA?. *MBA Central*. Accessed January 5, 2023, from https://www.mbacentral.org/economics-mba-degrees/.

Meley, C. (2022, April 22). Social impact MBA: Change the world through business. *MBA*. Accessed January 1, 2023, from https://www.mba.com/business-school-and-careers/career-possibilities/social-impact-mba.

Microsoft. (n.d.) *Executive officers*. Accessed January 7, 2023, from https://news.microsoft.com/exec/satya-nadella/.

MIT SLOAN. (2022). *2021–2022 MBA employment report*. Accessed January 7, 2023, from https://mitsloan.mit.edu/sites/default/files/2022-12/MBA-Employment-Report-2022-2023.pdf.

NYU Stern. (n.d.) *Economics*. Accessed January 5, 2023, from https://www.stern.nyu.edu/programs-admissions/full-time-mba/academics/specializations/economics.

Questrom School of Business. (n.d.) *Social impact MBA*. Accessed January 26, 2023, from https://www.bu.edu/questrom/degree-programs/full-time-mba/social-impact-mba/.

Rosenberg, E. (2022, December 27). Who is Sundar Pichai?. *Investopedia*. Accessed January 7, 2023, from https://www.investopedia.com/articles/investing/090815/look-sundar-pichai-googles-new-ceo.asp.

Sasu, D.D. (2022, November 18). Demographics of Nigeria - Statistics & facts. *Statista*. Accessed January 30, 2023, from https://www.statista.com/topics/6477/demographics-of-nigeria/#topicHeader__wrapper.

Schiller, B. (2011, January 17). The rise of the MBA politicians. *The Financial Times*. Accessed January 3, 2023, from https://www.ft.com/content/96d634f0-1ffd-11e0-a6fb-00144feab49a.

Schlegelmilch, B. B. (2022). *Global marketing strategy - An executive digest* (2nd ed.). Springer International Publishing.

Schlegelmilch, B. B., & Szőcs, I. (Eds.). (2020). *Rethinking business responsibility in a global context: Challenges to corporate social responsibility, sustainability and ethics*. Springer Nature.

Scott, A. (2021, December 11). Top 15 JD MBA programs and how to get into them. *Inspira Futures*. Accessed January 24, 2023, from https://www.inspirafutures.com/blog/top-15-jd-mba-programs#b3.

Sheehy, B., & Farneti, F. (2021). Corporate social responsibility, sustainability, sustainable development and corporate sustainability: What is the difference, and does it matter? *Sustainability, 13*(11), 5965.

The Economist. (2023, January 17). For the first time since the 1960s, China's population is shrinking. *The Economist*. Accessed January 26, 2023, from https://www.economist.com/china/2023/01/17/for-the-first-time-since-the-1960s-chinas-population-is-shrinking?utm_content=article-link-4&etear=nl_sunday_today_4&utm_campaign=r.the-economist-sunday-today&utm_medium=email.internal-newsletter.np&utm_source=salesforce-marketing-cloud&utm_term=1/22/2023&utm_id=1457320.

The Heller School at Brandeis University. (n.d.) *Social impact MBA*. Accessed January 26, 2023, from https://heller.brandeis.edu/mba/index.html.

TU Berlin. (n.d.) *Energy management MBA*. Accessed January 22, 2023, from https://master-in-energy.com/courses/energy-management/.

TUM. (n.d.) *Executive MBA in Business & IT*. Accessed January 7, 2023, from https://www.tum.de/en/studies/degree-programs/detail/executive-mba-in-business-it-master-of-business-administration-mba/.

UCLA Anderson School of Management. (n.d.) *Technology career path*. Accessed January 7, 2023, from https://www.anderson.ucla.edu/degrees/full-time-mba/career-impact/technology-career-path.

University of Cambridge. (n.d.). *The Cambridge MBA degree*: Curriculum. Accessed January 7, 2023, from https://www.jbs.cam.ac.uk/programmes/mba/curriculum/.

University of Minnesota. (n.d.) *Business Administration M.B.A.*. Accessed January 5, 2023, from https://onestop2.umn.edu/pcas/viewCatalogProgram.do?programID=7262.

University of Victoria. (n.d.). *MBA in sustainable innovation*. Accessed January 24, 2023, from https://www.uvic.ca/gustavson/gill/mba/index.php.

UNSW Sydney. (n.d.-a). *Master of Laws/MBA (Law)*. Accessed January 24, 2023, from https://www.unsw.edu.au/study/postgraduate/master-of-laws-business-administration-law?studentType=Domestic.

UNSW Sydney. (n.d.-b). *MBAX (Social impact)*. Accessed January 26, 2023, from https://www.unsw.edu.au/business/our-schools/agsm/learn-with-us/agsm-programs/mbax-social-impact.

Wingfield-Hayes, R. (2023, January 20). Japan was the future but it's stuck in the past. *BBC News*. Accessed January 26, 2023, from https://www.bbc.com/news/world-asia-63830490.

Appendix A: Financial Times Global MBA Ranking

MBA (Full-Time Programs) 2023 Ranking by the Financial Times[1]

#	School name	Location, by primary campus
1	Columbia Business School	US
2	INSEAD	France/Singapore
3	Iese Business School	Spain
4	Harvard Business School	US
4	Stanford Graduate School of Business	US
6	SDA Bocconi School of Management	Italy
7	University of California at Berkeley: Haas	US
8	Cornell University: Johnson	US
9	Northwestern University, Kellogg School of Management	US
10	Yale School of Management	US
11	Duke University's Fuqua School of Business	US
11	MIT: Sloan	US
11	University of Chicago: Booth	US
14	UCLA Anderson School of Management	US
15	Dartmouth College: Tuck	US

---

[1] Please be advised that the rankings are subject to annual updates. For the most up-to-date information, we suggest referring to the official website of the Financial Times.

#	School name	Location, by primary campus
16	London Business School	UK
17	HEC Paris	France
17	University of Virginia: Darden	US
19	New York University: Stern	US
20	CEIBS	China
21	University of Southern California: Marshall	US
22	IE Business School	Spain
23	University of Cambridge: Judge	UK
23	Shanghai University of Finance and Economics: College of Business	China
25	National University of Singapore Business School	Singapore
26	University of Michigan: Ross	US
27	ESCP Business School	France/Italy/Spain/UK/Germany
28	University of Oxford: Saïd	UK
29	Rice University: Jones	US
30	Esade Business School	Spain
31	Washington University: Olin	US
32	Georgetown University: McDonough	US
32	IMD — International Institute for Management Development	Switzerland
32	University of Washington: Michael G Foster	US
35	University of North Carolina: Kenan-Flagler	US
36	Emory University: Goizueta	US
37	Imperial College Business School	UK
38	Nanyang Business School, NTU Singapore	Singapore
39	Indian School of Business	India
40	University of Florida: Warrington	US
41	HKU Business School	Hong Kong
42	HKUST Business School	Hong Kong
43	Michigan State University: Broad	US
44	Vanderbilt University: Owen	US
45	University of Rochester: Simon Business School	US
46	Alliance Manchester Business School	UK
47	EDHEC Business School	France
48	Fudan University School of Management	China
49	Carnegie Mellon: Tepper	US
50	University of Texas at Austin: McCombs	US
51	Indian Institute of Management Ahmedabad	India
52	Indian Institute of Management Bangalore	India
53	Arizona State University: WP Carey	US
54	University of California at Irvine: Merage	US
55	Warwick Business School	UK

Appendix A: Financial Times Global MBA Ranking

#	School name	Location, by primary campus
56	Mannheim Business School	Germany
57	University of Maryland: Smith	US
58	George Washington University	US
59	University of Texas at Dallas: Jindal	US
59	University of St Gallen	Switzerland
61	University of Georgia: Terry	US
61	Singapore Management University: Lee Kong Chian	Singapore
63	Rotterdam School of Management, Erasmus University	Netherlands
64	CUHK Business School	Hong Kong
64	Georgia Tech Scheller College of Business	US
66	Bayes Business School (formerly Cass)	UK
67	University of Toronto: Rotman	Canada
68	WHU – Otto Beisheim School of Management	Germany
69	University of Massachusetts Amherst: Isenberg	US
70	ESSEC Business School	France/Singapore
71	Queen's University: Smith	Canada
71	University of Notre Dame: Mendoza	US
73	Boston College: Carroll	US
74	Texas A&M University: Mays	US
75	Boston University Questrom School of Business	US
76	EMLYON Business School	France
76	Indian Institute of Management Calcutta	India
78	Durham University Business School	UK
78	University of Pittsburgh: Katz	US
78	Northeastern University: D'Amore-McKim	US
81	William & Mary: Mason	US
82	Sungkyunkwan University GSB	South Korea
83	McGill University: Desautels	Canada
84	Western University: Ivey	Canada
85	The Lisbon MBA Catolica | Nova	Portugal
86	Audencia	France
87	Trinity College Dublin, Trinity Business School	Ireland
88	Cranfield School of Management	UK
89	Indian Institute of Management Indore	India
90	TIAS Business School, Tilburg University	Netherlands
90	Indian Institute of Management Lucknow	India
92	Brigham Young University: Marriott	US
93	Vlerick Business School	Belgium
94	University College Dublin: Smurfit	Ireland
95	AGSM at UNSW Business School	Australia
95	Babson College: Olin	US

Appendix A: Financial Times Global MBA Ranking

#	School name	Location, by primary campus
97	Birmingham Business School	UK
98	Frankfurt School of Finance and Management	Germany
99	University of California at Davis	US
100	Eada Business School Barcelona	Spain

Appendix B: Financial Times Global Executive MBA Ranking

Executive MBA 2022 Ranking by Financial Times[1]

#	School Name	Location
1	Kellogg/HKUST Business School	Hong Kong
2	CEIBS	China/Switzerland/Ghana
3	Tsinghua University/INSEAD	China/Singapore/France/UAE
4	HEC Paris	France/Qatar
5	ESCP Business School	France/Germany/Italy/Lebanon/Poland/Spain/UK
6	Trium: HEC Paris/LSE/NYU: Stern	France/US/UK/China
7	MIT: Sloan	US
8	University of Chicago: Booth	US/UK/Hong Kong
9	Washington University: Olin	China
10	IESE Business School	Spain/US
11	UCLA: Anderson/National University of Singapore	Singapore/US
12	IE Business School	Spain
12	Fudan University School of Management	China
14	Yale School of Management	US
15	University of Oxford: Saïd	UK
16	Kellogg/WHU Beisheim	Germany
17	INSEAD	France/Singapore/UAE

[1] Please be advised that the rankings are subject to annual updates. For the most up-to-date information, we suggest referring to the official website of the Financial Times.

© The Author(s), under exclusive license to Springer Nature Switzerland AG 2023
B. B. Schlegelmilch, G. D. Iliev, *The MBA Compass*,
https://doi.org/10.1007/978-3-031-42739-8

Appendix B: Financial Times Global Executive MBA Ranking

#	School Name	Location
18	HKU Business School	China
19	London Business School	UK/UAE
20	Arizona State University: WP Carey	China
21	UCLA Anderson School of Management	US
22	University of Pennsylvania: Wharton	US
23	Northwestern University, Kellogg School of Management	US
24	National University of Singapore Business School	Singapore
24	CUHK Business School	Hong Kong
26	Imperial College Business School	UK
27	IMD — International Institute for Management Development	Switzerland
27	ESSEC Business School/Mannheim Business School	France/Germany/Singapore
29	Yonsei University School of Business	South Korea
30	Kellogg/York University: Schulich	Canada
31	Koç University Graduate School of Business	Turkey
32	University of St Gallen	Switzerland
33	Singapore Management University: Lee Kong Chian	Singapore
34	SDA Bocconi School of Management	Italy
34	Warwick Business School	UK
36	Emory University: Goizueta	US
36	University of Cambridge: Judge	UK
38	University of Texas at Austin: McCombs	US
39	WU Vienna: Executive Academy/University of Minnesota: Carlson	Austria
40	New York University: Stern	US
40	IBS-Moscow Ranepa	Russia
42	Kedge Business School	France/China
43	ESMT Berlin	Germany
44	Kozminski University	Poland
44	Indian School of Business	India
46	BI Norwegian Business School/Fudan University School of Management	China
47	EMLYON Business School	France/China
47	Cornell University: Johnson/Queen's University: Smith	US/Canada
49	EDHEC Business School	France
50	Moscow School of Management Skolkovo	Russia
51	University of Michigan: Ross	US
52	Duke University's Fuqua School of Business	US

Appendix B: Financial Times Global Executive MBA Ranking

#	School Name	Location
53	University of Toronto: Rotman	Canada
54	Bayes Business School (formerly Cass)	UK/UAE
54	Georgetown University: McDonough	US
56	Antwerp Management School	Belgium
57	Stockholm School of Economics	Sweden
58	Rotterdam School of Management, Erasmus University	Netherlands
59	INCAE Business School	Costa Rica
60	University of Zurich	Switzerland
61	University of Washington: Michael G Foster	US
62	Copenhagen Business School	Denmark
62	Frankfurt School of Finance and Management	Germany
64	Trinity College Dublin, Trinity Business School	Ireland
65	Henley Business School	UK/Finland/Denmark
66	Vlerick Business School	Belgium
67	Monash Business School	Australia
68	Hult International Business School	US/UK/UAE
69	University College Dublin: Smurfit	Ireland
70	HEC Lausanne, University of Lausanne	Switzerland
71	Texas A&M University: Mays	US
71	University of Maryland: Smith	US
73	Rutgers Business School	US
74	UCT Graduate School of Business	South Africa
74	Georgia Tech Scheller College of Business	US
74	TBS Education	France/Morocco
74	Mannheim Business School	Germany
78	Neoma Business School	France/China/Iran
79	St Petersburg University, Graduate School of Management	Russia
80	Georgia State University: Robinson	US
80	TIAS Business School, Tilburg University	Netherlands
82	Queen's University: Smith	Canada
83	BI Norwegian Business School	Norway
84	The Lisbon MBA Catolica	Nova	Portugal
85	Michigan State University: Broad	US
86	University of Utah: David Eccles	US
86	Indian Institute of Management Bangalore	India
88	Aalto University	Finland
89	Western University: Ivey	Canada
89	Rennes School of Business	France/China

Appendix B: Financial Times Global Executive MBA Ranking

#	School Name	Location
91	University of Strathclyde Business School	UK/Greece/Malaysia/UAE/Oman/Bahrain
91	National Sun Yat-sen University	Taiwan
93	University of Tennessee: Haslam College of Business	US
94	Melbourne Business School	Australia
95	IPADE Business School	Mexico
95	Lancaster University Management School	UK/Ghana/Malaysia
97	Cranfield School of Management	UK
98	Politecnico di Milano School of Management	Italy
99	Audencia	France/Algeria
100	Fordham University: Gabelli	US

Appendix C: Triple Crown Accredited Business Schools

Triple Crown Accredited Business Schools 2023[1]

Argentina	IAE Business School, Universidad Austral
Australia	Monash Business School, Monash University
Australia	QUT Graduate School of Business, Queensland University of Technology
Australia	University of Sydney Business School
Austria	WU Executive Academy
Belgium	Vlerick Business School
Brazil	Fundação Getulio Vargas—FGV (EAESP)
Brazil	Insper—Instituto de Ensino e Pesquisa
Canada	HEC Montreal
Canada	Telfer School of Management, University of Ottawa
Chile	Universidad Adolfo Ibañez
China	Antai College of Economics and Management, Shanghai Jiao Tong University
China	Beijing Institute of Technology
China	Chongqing University
China	Lingnan (University) College, Sun Yat-sen University
China	Shanghai University of Finance and Economics, College of Business (SUFE)
China	Sun Yat-Sen University Business School

[1] Please be advised that the list is subject to updates. For the most up-to-date information, we suggest referring to the official websites of AACSB International, AMBA, and EQUIS.

Appendix C: Triple Crown Accredited Business Schools

China	University of International Business and Economics (UIBE)
China	Xiamen University
China	Zhejiang University, School of Management
China	Dalian University of Technology
China	Beijing Jiaotong University
China	Xi'an Jiaotong-Liverpool University
Hong Kong	Hong Kong Baptist University School of Business
Macao	University of Macau
Colombia	Universidad de Los Andes
Costa Rica	INCAE Business School
Denmark	Aarhus University School of Business and Social Sciences
Denmark	Copenhagen Business School
Egypt	The American University in Cairo
Finland	Aalto University School of Business
Finland	Hanken School of Economics
France	Audencia Business School
France	EDHEC Business School
France	EMLYON Business School
France	ESSCA School of Management
France	ESSEC Business School
France	Grenoble Graduate School of Business, Grenoble École de Management
France	HEC Paris
France	ICN Business School
France	IESEG School of Management
France	INSEAD
France	Kedge Business School
France	Montpellier Business School
France	NEOMA Business School
France	Rennes School of Business
France	Toulouse Business School (TBS Education)
France	Burgundy School of Business
France	Ecole de Management de Normandie
France	EM Strasbourg Business School
France	Groupe Sup de Co La Rochelle (NOW CALLED Excelia Group, La Rochelle Business School)
Germany	ESMT European School of Management and Technology
Germany	Mannheim Business School
Germany	TUM School of Management, Technische Universität München
Germany	Frankfurt School of Finance & Management
India	Indian Institute of Management Calcutta
India	Indian Institute of Management Indore
India	Indian School of Business
Ireland	Kemmy Business School, University of Limerick
Ireland	Trinity College Dublin School of Business

Appendix C: Triple Crown Accredited Business Schools

Ireland	UCD Michael Smurfit Graduate Business School, University College Dublin
Italy	Politecnico di Milano School of Management
Italy	SDA Bocconi
Japan	NUCB Business School, Nagoya University of Commerce & Business
Mexico	EGADE Business School
Mexico	IPADE Business School, Universidad Panamericana
Mexico	ITAM Instituto Tecnológico Autónomo de México
Netherlands	Faculty of Economics & Business, University of Amsterdam
Netherlands	Maastricht University School of Business and Economics
Netherlands	Rotterdam School of Management, Erasmus University
New Zealand	University of Auckland Business School
New Zealand	University of Canterbury, College of Business & Law
New Zealand	Victoria Business School, Victoria University of Wellington
New Zealand	Waikato Management School, University of Waikato
Norway	BI Norwegian Business School
Norway	NHH Norwegian School of Economics
Peru	CENTRUM Católica
Poland	Kozminski University
Poland	University of Warsaw Faculty of Management
Portugal	Católica Lisbon School of Business & Economics
Portugal	Nova School of Business and Economics
Singapore	Lee Kong Chian School of Business, Singapore Management University
Slovenia	Faculty of Economics, University of Ljubljana
South Africa	Gordon Institute of Business Science, University of Pretoria
South Africa	University of Cape Town Graduate School of Business
South Africa	University of Stellenbosch Business School
Spain	ESADE Business School
Spain	IE Business School
Sweden	University of Gothenburg School of Business, Economics & Law
Sweden	LUSEM—Lund University School of Economics and Management
Switzerland	IMD Business School
Switzerland	University of St. Gallen
Thailand	Thammasat Business School, Thammasat University
Thailand	Chulalongkorn Business School, Chulalongkorn University
Turkey	Graduate School of Business, Koç University
UK	Adam Smith Business School, University of Glasgow
UK	Alliance Manchester Business School, University of Manchester
UK	Aston Business School, Aston University

Appendix C: Triple Crown Accredited Business Schools

UK	Birmingham Business School, University of Birmingham
UK	Bayes Business School, City, University of London
UK	Cranfield School of Management
UK	Durham University Business School
UK	Henley Business School, University of Reading
UK	Imperial College Business School
UK	Kent Business School
UK	Lancaster University Management School
UK	Leeds University Business School
UK	London Business School
UK	Loughborough University School of Business and Economics
UK	Manchester Metropolitan University Business School
UK	Newcastle University Business School
UK	Nottingham University Business School
UK	Sheffield University Management School
UK	Strathclyde Business School, University of Stratchclyde
UK	The Open University Business School
UK	University of Bradford School of Management
UK	University of Edinburgh Business School
UK	University of Exeter Business School
UK	Warwick Business School, University of Warwick
UK	The University of Liverpool, Management School
UK	King's Business School, King's College London
USA	Hult International Business School (including Ashridge)
USA	Olin Business School, Washington University in St Louis
USA	Miami Herbert Business School, University of Miami

MIX
Papier aus verantwortungsvollen Quellen
Paper from responsible sources
FSC® C105338

If you have any concerns about our products,
you can contact us on
ProductSafety@springernature.com

In case Publisher is established outside the EU,
the EU authorized representative is:
**Springer Nature Customer Service Center GmbH
Europaplatz 3, 69115 Heidelberg, Germany**

Printed by Libri Plureos GmbH
in Hamburg, Germany